DAMSELS IN DISTRESS

DAMSELS IN DISTRESS

Biblical Solutions
for Problems Women Face

MARTHA PEACE

P&R
PUBLISHING
P.O. BOX 817 • PHILLIPSBURG • NEW JERSEY 08865-0817

Scripture quotations are from the NEW AMERICAN STANDARD BIBLE®. © Copyright The Lockman Foundation 1960, 1962, 1963, 1968, 1971, 1972, 1973, 1975, 1977, 1995. Used by permission.

Scripture quotations marked KJV are from The Holy Bible, King James Version.

Italics within Scripture quotations indicate emphasis added.

The appendix is reproduced with permission of Focus Publishing, Inc. Bemidji, MN, from the "Salvation Handbook," 2005.

Printed in the United States of America

Library of Congress Cataloging-in-Publication Data

Peace, Martha.
    Damsels in distress : biblical solutions for problems women face / Martha Peace.
        p. cm.
    Includes bibliographical references and index.
    ISBN-10: 1-59638-038-1 (paper)
    ISBN-13: 978-1-59638-038-7 (paper)
    1. Christian women—Religious life. 2. Christian life—Biblical teaching. I. Title.

BV4527.P395 2006
248.8'43—dc22

2006043289

To
Patty Thorn
because she shows her love for the Lord
by her servant's heart

Contents

8

List of Figures

Acknowledgments

Writing the acknowledgments has got to be the most fun part of writing a book. It is a joy to think back on all the help the Lord has given me through various people. First of all, my daughter, Anna Maupin, edited each chapter as it was written. There were times when I would go to her home and wash clothes and change diapers so that she could read. Anna has a gift from God to edit and somehow not change the author's style or theology. Anna not only edits the chapters but also manages to give you "hope" even with the most confusing paragraphs. (Sometimes I didn't even know what I was trying to say!)

My pastor, John Crotts, has helped with every book I have written. He came to our church at the end of *The Excellent Wife* project, and he was a huge blessing. Now we have a process. I write a chapter, give it to Anna, she makes it readable; next I correct it; then John reads it for theology and biblical accuracy. By the way, I don't even start writing a chapter until John and I have gone over the outline for that chapter first. We have learned "by the hardest" (as my grandmother used to say) that this prevents massive rewrites later.

Another one of my pastors read and made very helpful comments. Kent Keller was especially helpful in challenging me to clarify what I was trying to say. A previous pastor of mine was also greatly helpful. His name is Howard Dial, and he is my former pastor at Berachah Bible Church in Fayetteville, Georgia. Howard is a greatly gifted teacher and student of the Word. He graciously let me adapt some of his sermon material in the chapters on vanity and legalism. His material on those topics impacted me so much at the time that years later, as I was developing my material, I remembered his sermons. Howard gave me a copy of his sermons and was glad for me to use it.

Lou Priolo is a biblical counselor in Montgomery, Alabama, where he is on staff at Eastwood Presbyterian Church and is the director of Eastwood Counseling Ministries. Lou, along with Howard Eyrich, trained me in biblical counseling at the Atlanta Biblical Counseling Center. It was there that Lou taught me to counsel someone who was being manipulated or manipulative. I am grateful that Lou allowed me to adapt some of his material for this book.

Two friends of mine from California, Dr. Laura Hendrickson and Mary Sommerville, read the manuscript and provided very thoughtful and insightful suggestions. Thank you, Laura and Mary!

I also want to thank my friends from church, Brooke and Bill May, for proofreading the manuscript. When I made their corrections, I laughed at one sentence in particular. It was a compound sentence, and I had used the word *then* five times! Bill is a City of Atlanta firefighter and paramedic and a budding author. (Watch for his upcoming book.)

As always, my husband, Sanford, has been very encouraging and helpful throughout the process. He is my computer, I think, genius. Our son, David Peace, called while I was writing this and asked me what I was doing. So, I told him I was writing the acknowledgments and he replied, "You know how to spell my name, don't you?" Yes, as a matter of fact, I do! But the truth is he didn't do anything to help me with this book. Last, I want to thank Barbara Lerch, Tara Davis, and Marvin Padgett from P&R Publishing for their help and enthusiasm for this project.

Introduction

It is a sunny, warm day in Peachtree City, Georgia, and I am up early preparing for the ladies who will be in my home today for counseling. I run around making sure everything is reasonably straight and that there is extra toilet paper in the bathroom. The special hazelnut cream coffee that I love is brewing in the coffee maker. My favorite place to counsel is sitting around the kitchen table with my Bible, counseling notes, and coffee in front of me. Before anyone arrives, I have to remove the giant ceramic rooster that sits in the middle of the table so that we ladies can see each other. One of the women coming for counseling today is new to me so I do not know what her problem is—but the Lord does, and I have already asked Him for wisdom to help her.

It is almost always difficult for a new counselee to come to me (a stranger to her) and begin to tell personal details of her life and her problems. If the problem were not distressful for her, she would not even come. So, I try to make it as easy as I can by offering her coffee and trying to make her comfortable around the table. After some general chit-chat, I usually begin the counseling session with a question such as, "How can I help you?" As she talks to me, and I ask further questions, often I will know by the end of the first session what her problem is, what she has already done about it, and what she would like for me to do about it.

Damsels in Distress is about some of those problems. And even though a counselee may feel overwhelmed at the enormity of her problem, there is always a biblical solution. So, for the problems addressed in this book, my prayer for the ladies that sit around my kitchen table seeking biblical counsel, as well as the readers of this book, is that God will use these biblical principles and practical applications to greatly bless you and to glorify Himself.

1

Casting All My Cares on Whom?

Shortly before I became a Christian, I had so many problems that it would have been difficult to name them all. Afterward, I realized that my biggest problem had been solved because God had cleansed me from and forgiven me for my sin. It would be wonderful to report that from then on I had no problems. However, that's not true. Fortunately for me, God provided resources to help me either solve or cope with those problems. The resources were being a Christian, the Scriptures, learning about the character of God, and my friend, Katrina Barnes.

Being a Christian

At the moment I became a Christian, God supernaturally accomplished several things all at once. One accomplishment was that He cleansed me of my past, present, and future sins. Theologians call that Christ's substitutionary atoning work on the cross. In other words, the Lord Jesus Christ took the punishment for sin that I deserved and gave *me* credit for *His* righteousness.

All of us like sheep have gone astray,
Each of us has turned to his own way;

But the LORD has caused the iniquity of us all
To fall on Him. (Isa. 53:6)

He [God] made Him [Jesus Christ] who knew no sin to
be sin on our behalf, so that we might become the righteousness of God in Him. (2 Cor. 5:21)

I knew I did not earn or deserve my salvation, but that God
in His mercy had made me right with Him "as a gift by His grace
through the redemption which is in Christ Jesus . . ." (Rom.
3:24). (For a much more in-depth Bible study on how to become
a Christian, see the Appendix: Salvation Work Sheets.)

God also gave me a new heart so that I would not only
believe the gospel but also become aware of my sin, be motivated
to glorify God, and want to obey Him. The new heart is given by
the regenerating work of the Holy Spirit.

He saved us, not on the basis of deeds which we have
done in righteousness, but according to His mercy, by
the *washing of regeneration and renewing by the Holy
Spirit*, whom He poured out upon us richly through
Jesus Christ our Savior, so that being justified by His
grace we would be made heirs according to the hope of
eternal life. (Titus 3:5–7)

God literally indwells every believer to save them, help
them, and keep them in His care. For those who are Christians,
not only are their sins forgiven completely, but the grip that sin
had over them prior to salvation also has been broken. Now they
do not have to sin because God will supernaturally help them.
The Bible says that *we are no longer slaves to sin* (see Rom. 6:6).
Their motivation to solve problems biblically is out of *gratitude*

to the Lord for what He has done on the cross. Their lives and thus their approach to their problems are lived out for His glory.

> Therefore if anyone is in Christ, he is a new creature; the old things passed away; behold, new things have come. (2 Cor. 5:17)

Next to being a Christian, the most precious resource God gave to help me was the Scriptures.

The Scriptures

The Scriptures are God's Word, literally God-breathed, and profitable to teach us, correct us, and train us (see 2 Tim. 3:16–17). They are God's revelation of Himself to us. They contain God's commands and His encouragement. They tell us what He is like.

Reading the Bible as a new believer was amazing. Bible stories I had heard as a child took on new meaning. So did my problems. I found out that the Bible gives us very practical instruction on what to do about various problems. I discovered for the first time that I had real help and hope. As a new believer I worried that I would slip back into my old sins. What a tremendous relief it was when someone pointed out the following promise:

> No temptation has overtaken you but such as is common to man; and God is faithful, who will not allow you to be tempted beyond what you are able, but with the temptation will provide the way of escape also, so that you will be able to endure it. (1 Cor. 10:13)

The word for *temptation* in the Greek can also be translated *pressure* or *trial*. In other words, no *pressure* or *trial* has overtaken us except those common to others, and God is faithful to not allow us to be *pressured* or *tried* beyond what we are able to bear. He will ultimately provide a way of escape and in the meanwhile, give us grace to endure it. What a precious promise this is, written specifically to Christians to give us hope regardless of our circumstances!

Another special promise for Christians is found in Romans 8:28–30:

> And we know that God causes all things to work together for good to those who love God, to those who are called according to His purpose. For those whom He foreknew, He also predestined to become conformed to the image of His Son, so that He would be the firstborn among many brethren; and these whom He predestined, He also called; and these whom He called, He also justified; and these whom He justified, He also glorified.

Most of us are probably familiar with the promise that *God causes all things to work together for good*. What we might not be familiar with is the next phrase in that sentence—*to those who love God. Those who love God* are Christians who obey His Word. As a result, God somehow supernaturally uses good as well as bad circumstances to help mold us into Christlike character. There is nothing, however painful, that we must go through in vain. God will not only help us, but He will also use all things for our good and for His glory. What a comforting thought when we are in a trial or undergoing terrific pressure or temptation!

Learning about the Character of God

As a new believer, my pastor encouraged me to read A. W. Pink's book *The Attributes of God*. That book was a great blessing to me because it not only taught me about God's character but also helped me to begin to think through issues from the perspective of God's character. Instead of seeing my circumstances in a vacuum, I could remember, along with many of His other attributes, that God loved me, was compassionate, and was faithful to keep His promises. This always gave me hope even if my problem was not solved immediately.

God loves us.

> But God demonstrates His own love toward us, in that while we were yet sinners, Christ died for us. (Rom. 5:8)

> For I am convinced that neither death, nor life, nor angels, nor principalities, nor things present, nor things to come, nor powers, nor height, nor depth, nor any other created thing, will be able to separate us from the love of God, which is in Christ Jesus our Lord. (Rom. 8:38–39)

> See how great a love the Father has bestowed on us, that we would be called children of God; and such we are. For this reason the world does not know us, because it did not know Him. (1 John 3:1)

> We love, because He first loved us. (1 John 4:19)

God is compassionate.

> Therefore the LORD longs to be gracious to you,
> And there He waits on high to have compassion on you.
> For the LORD is a God of justice;
> How blessed are all those who long for Him. (Isa.
>   30:18)

> Seeing the people, He [the Lord Jesus] felt compassion
> for them, because they were distressed and dispirited like
> sheep without a shepherd. (Matt. 9:36)

> The LORD is compassionate and gracious,
> Slow to anger and abounding in lovingkindness. (Ps.
>   103:8)

> So then it does not depend on the man who wills or the
> man who runs, but on God who has mercy. (Rom. 9:16)

> But God, being rich in mercy, because of His great love
> with which He loved us, even when we were dead in our
> transgressions, made us alive together with Christ. . . .
> (Eph. 2:4–5)

God is faithful.

> God is faithful, through whom you were called into fel-
> lowship with His Son, Jesus Christ our Lord. (1 Cor. 1:9)

> Faithful is He who calls you, and He also will bring it to
> pass. (1 Thess. 5:24)

If we are faithless, He remains faithful, for He cannot
deny Himself. (2 Tim. 2:13)

Let us hold fast the confession of our hope without
wavering, for He who promised is faithful. (Heb. 10:23)

Therefore, those also who suffer according to the will of
God shall entrust their souls to a faithful Creator in
doing what is right. (1 Peter 4:19)

Learning about God and what He is like gave me greater sta-
bility and hope in my walk with the Lord. It gave me a compass
to guide me as I thought through problems. And then God gave
me another resource to cope, my friend Katrina.

The Wounds of a Friend

Katrina was my office mate when she and I taught nursing at
a local college. She and her church family prayed for my salvation for the entire first year we worked together. In addition,
Katrina witnessed to me on a regular basis. Instead of politely listening to her, I thought she was a nut, and I made my belief
abundantly clear! She would often go home in tears, get all
"prayed up," and come back the next day talking about the Lord
again. Being in that office with her was like being chained to the
apostle Paul.

After the Lord saved me (Katrina said that was the happiest
day of her life!), I wanted to hear what she knew about the Lord.
She began to teach me many wonderful, precious truths from
the Scriptures—and then one day something unusual happened.
We had completed a day with nursing students at the hospital,
and she walked up to me in the parking lot of the hospital with

her Bible in hand. She said, "I need to tell you something." So, we got in the car, and she read me the following verse:

> Faithful are the wounds of a friend,
> But deceitful are the kisses of an enemy. (Prov. 27:6)

I had never heard that before, and I asked, "What does that mean?" She explained that a true friend will tell you the truth even if it *wounds* or hurts you, but an enemy will only tell you what you want to hear. She said, "I have to tell you something."

Perceiving it wasn't going to be good news and probably rolling my eyes, I said, "What . . . ?" Then she told me that as a Christian now I had to stop doing or saying whatever it was I had done wrong that particular day. Not wanting to believe her, I said, "Show me in the Bible." Well, Katrina was armed and ready. She showed me verses and gently taught me not only that day but also many other days the basic biblical truths I needed to know. She was, and still is to me, a remarkably faithful friend.

Katrina's *wounds* temporarily embarrassed me, but I knew she was right, and I wanted so badly to honor the Lord that I saw them as good for me and realized that she really did love me. It was humbling, but God poured out His grace on me and helped me to learn and grow in His grace. Since then, God has given me a desire to be this kind of true friend to other women and to teach them what He has taught me. That's why I wrote this book.

There may be times as you read parts of this book that you will feel uncomfortable or even embarrassed as you see how God wants you to respond in a different way to a particular problem. If that happens, pray and seek refuge in the Lord, and He will help you and give you grace to change your thoughts or actions so that you may better give Him glory.

If you become discouraged, it may help to turn back to this page and remind yourself of the following verses:

> "Come unto Me [the Lord Jesus Christ], all who are weary and heavy-laden, and I will give you rest. Take My yoke upon you and learn from Me, for I am gentle and humble in heart, and YOU WILL FIND REST FOR YOUR SOULS. For My yoke is easy and My burden is light." (Matt. 11:28–30)

> But if any of you lacks wisdom, let him ask of God, who gives to all generously and without reproach, and it will be given to him. (James 1:5)

> "Peace I [the Lord Jesus Christ] leave with you; My peace I give to you; not as the world gives do I give to you. Do not let your heart be troubled, nor let it be fearful." (John 14:27)

> "Do not fear, for I am with you;
> Do not anxiously look about you, for I am your God.
> I will strengthen you, surely I will help you,
> Surely I will uphold you with My righteous right hand.
>   (Isa. 41:10)

> But as for me, the nearness of God is my good; . . .
> That I may tell of all Your works. (Ps. 73:28)

> God is our refuge and strength,
> A very present help in trouble. (Ps. 46:1)

This I recall to my mind,
Therefore I have hope. The LORD's lovingkindnesses
    indeed never cease,
For His compassions never fail.
They are new every morning;
Great is Your faithfulness.
"The LORD is my portion," says my soul,
"Therefore I have hope in Him." (Lam. 3:21–24)

Trust in the LORD with all your heart
And do not lean on your own understanding.
In all your ways acknowledge Him,
And He will make your paths straight. (Prov. 3:5–6)

The LORD is my shepherd,
I shall not want.
He makes me lie down in green pastures;
He leads me beside quiet waters.
He restores my soul;
He guides me in the paths of righteousness
For His name's sake. (Ps. 23:1–3)

Therefore, since we have a great high priest who has passed through the heavens, Jesus the Son of God, let us hold fast our confession. For we do not have a high priest who cannot sympathize with our weakness, but One who has been tempted in all things as we are, yet without sin. Therefore let us draw near with confidence to the throne of grace, so that we may receive mercy and find grace to help in time of need. (Heb. 4:14–16)

Conclusion

Just because I had become a Christian did not mean that I did not have problems. I still do, as a matter of fact! It was an incredible relief and joy, however, to discover that God had provided resources to help me. Being a Christian gave me an entirely new perspective on life. The Scriptures became a light to guide me as I searched them to find answers. Thinking about the character of God comforted me and gave me great hope. And last, but not least, God provided my friend Katrina to teach me and disciple me. She is my true friend.

As we seek comfort and refuge in the Lord to cope and learn how to solve the problems addressed in this book, God promises to give us grace to help us if we humble ourselves before Him. He is the one upon whom we can cast all of our cares.

Therefore humble yourselves under the mighty hand of God, that He may exalt you at the proper time, casting all your anxiety on Him, *because He cares for you.*
(1 Peter 5:6–7)

PART ONE

৩৫

Biblical Solutions for Problems with Others

৩৫

"Let all that you do be done in love."
1 Corinthians 16:14

2

Well, Isn't It OK If My Mother Told Me?

GOSSIP AND SLANDER

"Pssst! Come here. I want to tell you something, but you have to promise not to tell anyone." "Have you heard?" "Guess what!" "I couldn't believe she did. . . ." "I was shocked to learn. . . ." "I'm not supposed to tell, but we need to be praying for. . . ."

Gossip and slander. We are drawn to it like ants to a picnic. Whether it is young men standing around a water cooler at work or your mother telling you in a telephone conversation, gossip and slander are common sinful afflictions. And I do mean sinful *afflictions*. They destroy friendships, decimate reputations, and dishonor our Lord. They split churches, saturate public opinion, and sabotage our Christian witness.

The sins of gossip and slander are so offensive to God that there is a very graphic picture of the people who participated in these sins described in Psalm 35:15–16. In this psalm, King David implores God to "rescue my soul from their ravages" (v. 17). David was the Lord's anointed king, and his enemies attacked him every way they could, including using slander and gossip. Take a minute to visualize the grotesque word picture that David presents:

> But at my stumbling they rejoiced and gathered them-
>   selves together;
> The smiters whom I did not know gathered together
>   against me,
> They slandered me without ceasing.
> *Like godless jesters at a feast,*
> *They gnashed at me with their teeth.* (Ps. 35:15–16)

Unfortunately, we do not have to be a sworn enemy of God's kingdom to look like David's enemies.

Because gossip and slander are so much worse than we like to think, and because they are such "ugly" sins, we need to address them. We'll begin with a biblical explanation of gossip and slander, next we will look at the warnings and principles given to us in Scripture concerning gossip and slander, and last, we'll see what to put in their place.

What Are Gossip and Slander?

The Greek word for *gossip* is *diabolos*. We get our English word *devil* from *diabolos*. It means to accuse or to give false information. Somewhat related is the Greek word for slander—*blasphēmia*. We get our English word *blaspheme* from *blasphēmia*. It means evil speaking or vilification (to malign or disparage).

From Scripture, it is clear that both gossip and slander are sins. So clear, in fact, that there are many warnings against them:

> "You shall not go about as a slanderer among your peo-
> ple, and you are not to act against the life of your neigh-
> bor; I am the LORD." (Lev. 19:16)

Whoever secretly slanders his neighbor, him I will
     destroy;
No one who has a haughty look and an arrogant heart
     will I endure. (Ps. 101:5)

He who goes about as a slanderer reveals secrets,
Therefore do not associate with a gossip. (Prov. 20:19)

And He [the Lord Jesus] was saying, "That which pro-
ceeds out of the man, that is what defiles the man. For
from within, out of the heart of men, proceed the evil
thoughts . . . slander. . . . All these evil things proceed
from within and defile the man." (Mark 7:20–23)

Being characterized as a gossip or a slanderer describes a sinful,
unclean person. The warnings are strong and straightforward in
the Scriptures. Both gossip and slander entail passing on a bad
report about someone else. What is said may be true, or a lie, or
a mixture of both. *Even if it is true, the gossip or slanderer is
telling the wrong person.* (The only person they should be telling
is the person himself!)

To understand better the problems associated with gossip
and slander, let's consider the following seventeen biblical
principles:

1. *Gossip and slander characterize those whom God has
turned over to their own depravity:*

And just as they did not see fit to acknowledge God any
longer, God gave them over to a depraved mind, to do
those things which are not proper, being filled with all
unrighteousness, wickedness, greed, evil; full of envy,

murder, strife, deceit, malice; they are *gossips, slanderers*, haters of God, insolent, arrogant, boastful, inventors of evil, disobedient to parents, without understanding, untrustworthy, unloving, unmerciful; and although they know the ordinance of God, that those who practice such things are worthy of death, they not only do the same, but also give hearty approval to those who practice them. (Rom. 1:28–32)

According to Romans 1, people who reject the revelation God has given them by way of the creation, who do not give God the honor He is due, and who are not grateful to God are turned over to their depravity by God. Depravity is the thoroughly sinful state all people are born in. Being "turned over" means an unbeliever's sin is somewhat unrestrained by God. One of the evidences in the life of a person like this is that they gossip and slander.

2. *In the last days before Christ returns, men will be characterized as malicious gossips:*

But realize this, that in the last days difficult times will come. For men will be lovers of self, lovers of money, boastful, arrogant, revilers, disobedient to parents, ungrateful, unholy, unloving, irreconcilable, *malicious gossips*, without self-control, brutal, haters of good, treacherous, reckless, conceited, lovers of pleasure rather than lovers of God, holding to a form of godliness, although they have denied its power. . . . (2 Tim. 3:1–5)

The days before the Lord Jesus returns are now! Recently I learned of a court case in which a young husband got on the stand to testify against his wife in a divorce situation. He swore before God to tell the truth, and yet for twenty minutes he told one lie after another. His testimony was malicious, extremely self-serving, and incredibly slanderous. Unfortunately, he typifies people in these days. When you hear stories like this and think about how his wife must have felt, it's no wonder the apostle John wrote at the end of the book of Revelation, "Come, Lord Jesus!" (Rev. 22:20) The days before our Lord comes back are populated by men and women characterized as malicious gossips.

3. *Strong warnings go to those characterized by gossip and slander:*

> For I am afraid that perhaps when I come I may find you to be not what I wish and may be found by you to be not what you wish; that perhaps there will be strife, jealousy, angry tempers, disputes, *slanders, gossip,* arrogance, disturbances; I am afraid that when I come again my God may humiliate me before you, and I may mourn over many of those who have sinned in the past and not repented of the impurity, immorality and sensuality which they have practiced. (2 Cor. 12:20–21)

Oh my, did Paul have problems with the people in the church in Corinth! He poured his life into them for eighteen months, and after he left he received reports of their sinfully immature behavior. Paul intended to come back to Corinth and help them, but in the meantime he wrote with every bit of his full apostolic authority this warning: "it is *in the sight of God* that we have been speaking in Christ; and all for your upbuilding, beloved" (2 Cor. 12:19). Apparently the mix of sin, tempers, and strife that was rampant throughout the church was being fueled by their gossip and slander.

4. People who slander are described in the Bible as fools:

> He who conceals hatred has lying lips,
> And he who spreads *slander* is a fool.
> When there are many words, transgression is unavoidable,
> But he who restrains his lips is wise. (Prov. 10:18–19)

Fools are described in many ways in Scripture. We know that they won't listen, you can't reprove them, they make foolish decisions, they are oblivious to their own sin, they talk too much (often about things they know nothing or little about), they listen only to one side of the story, and they spread slander.

5. The Lord Jesus Christ included slander in a long list of evil things that defile us:

> But the things that proceed out of the mouth come from
> the heart, and those defile the man. For out of the heart
> come evil thoughts, murders, adulteries, fornications,
> thefts, false witness, *slanders*. These are the things which
> defile the man. . . . (Matt. 15:18–20)

The Pharisees believed that eating with a Gentile or not washing your hands according to their ceremonial traditions made you sinfully unclean. The Lord Jesus Christ refuted their self-righteous ritualistic beliefs by explaining that it is not what you touch outwardly that defiles you but what is in your heart (what you think and what you desire). One manifestation of the evil in your heart that eventually comes out of your mouth is slander.

6. We are to put off slander:

> But now you also, put them all aside: anger, wrath, mal-
> ice, *slander,* and abusive speech from your mouth. Do

> not lie to one another, since you laid aside the old self
> with its evil practices, and have put on the new self who
> is being renewed to a true knowledge according to the
> image of the One who created him. (Col. 3:8–10)

Paul explained to the church members in Colossae that as
Christians they were no longer to "walk" (think and act) as they
did when they were unsaved. They were now responsible to
become discerning about their sin, confess it as sin, and put off
the slanderous ways in which they used to think and speak before
they were Christians.

7. *Legalists slander those who do not uphold their standards:*

> But if anyone says to you, "This is meat sacrificed to idols,"
> do not eat it, for the sake of the one who informed you, and
> for conscience' sake; I mean not your own conscience, but
> the other man's; for why is my freedom judged by anoth-
> er's conscience? If I partake with thankfulness, why am I
> *slandered* concerning that for which I give thanks?
>
> Whether, then, you eat or drink or whatever you do,
> do all to the glory of God. (1 Cor. 10:28–31)

The legalist creates "thus saith the Lord" standards that are
above and beyond God's clear standards in the Scriptures. Paul
personally was slandered because he ate meat that was sacrificed
to idols. While it's fine to have your own personal standards, it is
not fine to unbiblically judge and slander others who do not
hold to the same guidelines.

8. *A slanderer will separate good friends:*

> A perverse man spreads strife,
> And a *slanderer* separates intimate friends. (Prov. 16:28)

Proverbs are those "oh, so true" sayings that generally will happen. Lies, innuendos, bad reports, and slander can most definitely ruin a perfectly good friendship! I know of one young man who was interested romantically in a particular young woman, and they became friends. He pulled away from her, though, after another one of his friends passed on a bad report about her. She could not understand why he pulled away, so she asked him. Confused, he decided to check out the facts. The facts ended up being in her favor, and now they are happily married. Fortunately for that couple, the slanderer did not succeed in separating them at the friendship stage of their relationship.

9. *If you do not want your secrets told, do not associate with a gossip:*

> He who goes about as a *slanderer* reveals secrets,
> Therefore do not associate with a *gossip*. (Prov. 20:19)

Thinking about not wanting your secrets told reminds me of the story of Samson. Delilah was finally able to sweet talk Samson out of the secret of his great strength. He confided in her, and she revealed his secret to his enemy, the Philistines. The rest is history, as they say, and Samson was overcome by his enemies (Judg. 16). Certainly not everyone is as calculating and deliberately malicious as Delilah when they tell others your secrets, but Scripture warns not to associate with such people (whether they intend malice or not).

10. *A righteous man speaks truth in his heart and does not slander:*

> O LORD, who may abide in Your tent?
> Who may dwell on Your holy hill?

He who walks with integrity, and works righteousness,
And speaks truth in his heart.
He does not *slander* with his tongue,
Nor does evil to his neighbor,
Nor takes up a reproach against his friend. (Ps. 15:1–3)

In Psalm 15, David describes several characteristics of a righteous man. Two of those characteristics are that he speaks truth in his heart and he does not slander. There is a direct relationship between what is in our hearts and what comes out of our mouths. The Lord Jesus explained the connection this way: "For the mouth speaks out of that which fills the heart. The good man brings out of his good treasure what is good; and the evil man brings out of his evil treasure what is evil" (Matt. 12:34–35). A godly man does not slander others secretly (in his heart) or openly (with his words).

11. *We are always to have exemplary behavior so that God will be glorified by those who slander us*:

Keep your behavior excellent among the Gentiles, so that in the thing in which they *slander* you as evildoers, they may because of your good deeds, as they observe them, glorify God in the day of visitation. (1 Peter 2:12)

God knew that the original recipients of Peter's letter were soon to undergo persecution by the wicked Roman King Nero. This inspired letter was a plea for them to prepare their minds and their hope, to be firm in their faith, to entrust their souls, to be ready always, to live for the will of God, and to keep their behavior excellent. We, too, should be ready and prepared by living a holy life. Then if we suffer at the hands of unbelievers' slander, we can know that we have honored God during persecution.

12. *Maintain a good conscience when slandered and, in so doing, you will be suffering for righteousness' sake:*

> But even if you should suffer for the sake of righteousness, you are blessed. AND DO NOT FEAR THEIR INTIMIDATION, AND DO NOT BE TROUBLED, but sanctify Christ as Lord in your hearts, always being ready to make a defense to everyone who asks you to give an account for the hope that is in you, yet with gentleness and reverence; and keep a good conscience so that in the thing in which you are *slandered*, those who revile your good behavior in Christ will be put to shame. For it is better, if God should will it so, that you suffer for doing what is right rather than for doing what is wrong. (1 Peter 3:14–17)

Often slander has at least a grain of truth in it. For example, it might be said of a certain woman that she is a bad mother. Well, she may not be the worst mother in the history of the world, but she may be harsh and selfish at times. So, there is some truth in saying she is a bad mother. Peter urges us to obey God and to have a clear conscience so that when we are slandered there won't be even a grain of truth in it. Instead, the slanderer will bring shame upon himself, and you will be suffering for righteousness' sake.

13. *When slandered we are to try to conciliate (gain the other person's goodwill):*

> When we are *slandered*, we try to conciliate; we have become as the scum of the world, the dregs of all things, even until now. (1 Cor. 4:13)

In 1 Corinthians 4, Paul gives very practical advice. He says, "when reviled . . . then bless," "when persecuted . . . then endure," and "when slandered . . . then conciliate." To try and gain the other person's goodwill, our responses are to be gracious and patient. If possible, talk to the slanderer and humbly try to understand his or her point. Finally, in a kind tone of voice explain the truthful view. This reminds me of what Paul wrote in Romans 12:18: "If possible, so far as it depends on you, be at peace with all men." When you are slandered, return good for evil and try to conciliate.

14. *One of the virtuous qualities of women is refraining from gossip:*

> Women must likewise be dignified, not malicious gossips, but temperate, faithful in all things. (1 Tim. 3:11)

Christian women who gossip about other people's problems or character flaws cannot be trusted to serve, especially in areas of the church in which she might be privy to sensitive information. She must, as Paul wrote, be faithful in all things, including the use of her tongue.

15. *Spiritually mature older women who are qualified to teach the younger women are not malicious gossips:*

> Older women likewise are to be reverent in their behavior, *not malicious gossips* nor enslaved to much wine, teaching what is good. (Titus 2:3)

Imagine a younger woman who struggles with some problem in her marriage or with her children. She is bewildered and embarrassed and does not know what to do. She privately approaches an older woman in church for advice. The next thing the younger woman knows is that everyone knows! It is easy to see why Paul instructed Titus to teach the older women that they were not to be malicious gossips.

16. *Younger widows are to remarry rather than have idle time to gossip:*

> At the same time they [younger widows] also learn to be idle, as they go around from house to house; and not merely idle, but also *gossips* and busybodies, talking about things not proper to mention. (1 Tim. 5:13)

In Paul's day life expectancy was short. And so, there were probably a lot of widows of all ages in the church. What was to be done with these women? Paul warns of the dangers of the less mature younger widows having too much time on their hands and engaging in gossip. Instead, he instructs them to remarry and, thus, keep busy and not have time to talk about improper topics.

17. *Christians are to replace slander with kindness, compassion, and forgiveness:*

> Let all bitterness and wrath and anger and clamor and *slander* be put away from you, along with all malice. Be kind to one another, tender-hearted, forgiving each other, just as God in Christ also has forgiven you. (Eph. 4:31–32)

When does a liar stop being a liar? When he starts telling the whole truth. When does a bitter, angry, malicious slanderer stop being a bitter, angry, malicious slanderer? When she starts being a kind, tender-hearted, and compassionate truth teller. God, in His great grace, helps us to turn from sinful habits to godly habits as our minds are renewed through the study and application of the Scriptures. Instead of "I hate him for what he did and I'm going to tell anyone who will listen," it's "What he did was wrong, but he has no capacity to love others as he should because he is an unbeliever." Christians are to honor God with their thoughts. They will never stop being slanders until they start being kind, compassionate, and tenderhearted.

From these biblical principles we see that there are not only strong warnings to the gossip and slanderer but also exhortations to put off these sins in our hearts and in our words. Lest we be like the rebellious children of Zion who "have taught their tongue to speak lies; [and] . . . weary themselves committing iniquity" (Jer. 9:5), let's turn our attention to the practical matter of putting off gossip and slander and putting on godly, righteous thoughts and words.

Put on a Heart of . . .

Sin begins in our hearts. We think sinful thoughts because that is our natural bent. The Bible does not command us to change our feelings; it commands us to renew our minds (Rom. 12:2). We do this by simply studying, meditating on, and memorizing the Bible, as well as by hearing it preached. Then when we realize that our thoughts and (gossiping and slanderous) speech are wrong, we are responsible to *change* our thoughts and speech. This is what Paul calls "lay[ing] aside the old self . . ." and "put[ting] on the new self"(see Eph. 4:22–24).

Everyone knows that bad habits are hard to break. However, Christians have the help of the Holy Spirit to convict and enable them to work on changing the sinful habit. Eventually righteous thoughts and actions will come to mind first rather than last.

Think about your own thoughts and words as you consider the examples of "putting off" and "putting on" in Fig. 2.1.

To change your sinful habit of gossiping and slandering, you must work hard, for as long as it takes, thinking righteous thoughts. This is not easy, but with God's help you can stop gossiping and slandering.

Conclusion

What James wrote is very sobering: "But no one can tame the tongue; it is a restless evil and full of deadly poison. With it

Fig. 2.1 Putting Off and Putting On

Put Off	Put On
1. "I'm not supposed to tell but . . ."	1. "I'm not supposed to tell so I am simply going to stop talking and pray for the person I was about to slander."
2. "I can't wait to tell my girlfriend what that other person did!"	2. "What the other person did was wrong, so I am going to go to her and try to help her. No one else need ever know." (Matt. 18:15)
3. "It makes me so angry what she did to her friend . . ." (then the phone rings, and it's your Mother).	3. "I feel angry but 'the anger of man does not achieve the righteousness of God' so I am going to pray for her and I am going to try, 'with grace,' to give her the gospel (James 1:20; Col. 4:6). My mother doesn't need to know."
4. "That former relative of mine hurt our family. This other person is asking about her, and I am going to tell every sordid detail!"	4. "Even though my former relative was and still is unrepentant, I am going to show love to her by not continuing to 'take into account a wrong suffered' and not replaying the sordid details over and over in my mind and out loud" (1 Cor. 13:5).
5. "What I am about to say is true so it is all right to say it."	5. "What I am about to say may be true, but I am still unnecessarily about to pass along a bad report. I need to change the topic of conversation so I won't be tempted to gossip" (Phil. 4:8).
6. "I know I haven't heard the other side of this story, but I'm sure what I'm hearing is accurate."	6. "I know I haven't heard the other side of this story, and I can't be sure what I should think until I hear the other side, so I better be careful what I say."

we bless our Lord and Father, and with it we curse men, who
have been made in the likeness of God. . . . My brethren these
things ought not to be this way" (James 3:8–10). This pro-
nouncement is really discouraging, but there is hope because
James goes on to write, "But He gives a greater grace . . ."
(James 4:6). We don't have to live a life characterized by slander and gossip because of God's grace. And how we thank God
for that grace!

What do your thoughts and words look like to God? Are you
like David's enemies who looked like "godless jesters at a feast"
as they gnashed their teeth and slandered him continually, or are
you like the Christian man or woman James describes who bri-
dles his tongue and does not speak against his brother (see Ps.
35:15–16; James 3:2; 4:11)? What is your prayer?

Study Questions

1. What are the Greek words for *gossip* and *slander*? What
do the Greek words mean? What English words are derived
from the Greek words?

2. According to Mark 7:20–23, from where does slander
originate?

3. Instead of passing on a bad report about someone, who is
the one person you *should* tell?

4. Match the following statements and Scriptures:

God gave them over to a depraved mind.	2 Corinthians 12:20–21
Men will be malicious gossips in the days before the Lord Jesus returns.	Matthew 15:18–20
Paul wrote a letter warning them of their gossip and slander.	Proverbs 10:18–19
One who spreads slander is a fool.	Romans 1:28–32
The Lord Jesus said that slander defiles a person.	2 Timothy 3:1–5

5. Make a list from Colossians 3:8–10 of what Christians are to *put aside*.

6. According to principle 7, what do legalism and slander have to do with each other?

7. What do we learn about a slanderer in Proverbs 16:28 and 20:19?

8. Where does the righteous man speak truth (Ps. 15:1–3)?

9. When someone slanders us, how should we react (see 1 Peter 2:12; 3:14–17)?

10. What does the word *conciliate* mean (see 1 Cor. 4:13)?

11. Match the following Scriptures concerning women and gossip:

Women are to be faithful in all things and not malicious gossips.	1 Timothy 5:13
Older women are to teach the younger women and not be a gossip themselves.	1 Timothy 3:11
Younger widows are not to be busybodies and gossips.	Titus 2:3

12. According to Ephesians 4:31–32, what should replace slander?

13. It is easy to be convicted of gossip and slander. However, it is not easy to break a sinful habit. It takes work and God's grace. Refer to the chart on page 42 and write out some of your typical wrong thoughts and the corresponding biblical "put-ons." Think and pray about this now so that the next time you are tempted you will be able to respond in a God-honoring way.

3

What Do You Mean I Can Live without Him?

IDOLATROUS EMOTIONAL ATTACHMENTS

The parents of twenty-two-year-old Wendy go to visit her over the Christmas holiday. Wendy is living and working in a large city several hours drive from their home. While there, Wendy's boyfriend, Jim, is present pretty much all of the time, except when he is at work or sleeping. Wendy's parents become concerned about, and then alarmed by, how Jim treats Wendy. He is unkind in his tone of voice, and over time they note that he is very uncomfortable talking about the Lord. The church he attends is not doctrinally sound, and he only goes occasionally. Also Jim takes license with drinking wine to the point of being drunk. Wendy's parents are puzzled as to why Wendy would desire (or tolerate) a boyfriend with such behavior. They pray about it and then talk with her privately. Even though Wendy and her parents have always had a good relationship, they are very surprised when she becomes defensive about her relationship with

Jim. She cries and becomes angry, and threatens to shut them out of her world if they do not accept Jim.

Bob's sister, Nancy, and her husband, Fred, invite Bob to visit them over spring break. Bob is a graduate student at a large university near them. Bob asks if he can bring his good friend, John, along. Nancy and Fred are glad to have Bob's friend. In fact, they have two spare bedrooms so sleeping arrangements will not be a problem. When Bob and John arrive, it is obvious that they are very close. So close, in fact, that Nancy and Fred become concerned. The way Bob and John look at each other and sit close together is more like boyfriend and girlfriend than simply friends. At night each settles into his own bedroom, but Fred happened to be up early one morning and saw John sneaking out of Bob's room. It certainly looked as if the two men had slept together. Nancy and Fred discuss what to do and decide to confront Bob privately. When they do, though, Bob explodes in anger and says he is not going to give up his relationship with John, and that they are being judgmental and are overreacting.

What do these two very different yet troubling relationships have in common? There is an idolatrous emotional bond that involves inordinate longings and sinful desires to be with the person even if it is obviously wrong. These desires have resulted in Wendy and Bob being willing to sin in order to continue their relationship with the other person. Wendy and Jim are having sex. Bob and John are in an active homosexual relationship. Both Wendy and Bob are willing to forsake their families, and even the Lord, if need be, to hang onto their lovers. How could this have happened? Both Wendy and Bob grew up in church and still profess to know the Lord. In this chapter we will consider what happened in their lives that caused them to end up like this. We will begin with a definition of idolatrous emotional attachments and then describe what these attachments are like. Next, we will consider how one is drawn into such a relationship and how, by God's grace, to renew your mind and turn *from* an idolatrous emotional attachment *to* a pure heart's worship of God.

What Are Idolatrous Emotional Attachments?

Idolatrous emotional attachments are those relationships that involve inordinate emotional longings for another person and a belief that you cannot live without them. These relationships often involve sexual immorality. Because of the sin involved, the emotions are excessive and seemingly very difficult to overcome. The sinning person's conscience is assuaged by thinking, *But we love each other*, or *No one will ever know*, or *God understands*, or *We won't do it again.* Their partner in sin really becomes their god as they are much more loyal to their partner than to the Lord Jesus. Their passionate desire for the illicit lover grows in proportion to how their love (if ever there really was love) for the Lord Jesus wanes. Often they realize that the relationship is not good, but there is just something that causes them to stick it out. Because anyone is capable of any sin the question becomes:

How Is Someone Drawn into This Kind of Relationship?

It is common for the person drawing you into such a relationship to say things such as, "No one ever understood me the way you do," or "I can't live without you," or "If you only knew what I have done, you wouldn't be my friend," or "I'm not sure what I would do if you ever left me" (hinting at suicide), or "I know we went too far this time but don't tell anybody. We won't do it again." Because we are often undiscerning and naive, we may be flattered into believing that they really do need us, and that we are responsible to help them, or that we can somehow change things for the better. Even Christian women's friendships can become idolatrous if one places the other ahead of her relationship with the Lord, her husband, or her children. As people weave their way into our lives and into our hearts, we override our concerns because of our own sinful desires or lusts.

"But each one is tempted when he is carried away and enticed by his own lust" (James 1:14). The word *lust* in this verse is the Greek word *epithumia*. *Epithumia* "denotes a strong desire of any kind."[1] The desire may be good, such as the desire the Lord Jesus had to eat the Passover with His apostles in Luke 22:15, or such as the desire that the apostle Paul had to depart from this life and be with the Lord in Philippians 1:23. On the other hand, the desire may be sinful. Consider the following Scriptures:

- Therefore do not let sin reign in your mortal body so that you obey its *lusts*. (Rom. 6:12)
- But put on the Lord Jesus Christ, and make no provision for the flesh in regard to its *lusts*. (Rom. 13:14)
- But I say, walk by the Spirit, and you will not carry out the *desire* of the flesh. (Gal. 5:16)
- Now those who belong to Christ Jesus have crucified the flesh with its passions and *desires*. (Gal. 5:24)
- Among them we too all formerly lived in the *lusts* of our flesh, indulging the desires of the flesh and of the mind, and were by nature children of wrath, even as the rest. (Eph. 2:3)
- For speaking out arrogant words of vanity they entice by fleshly *desires*, by sensuality, those who barely escape from the ones who live in error, promising them free-

dom while they themselves are slaves of corruption; for by what a man is overcome, by this he is enslaved. (2 Peter 2:18–19)

- For all that is in the world, the *lust* of the flesh and the *lust* of the eyes and the boastful pride of life, is not from the Father, but is from the world. (1 John 2:16)

However well-meaning or innocent we are when we begin a relationship, our own sinful desires draw us in and compel us to stay even if it is clearly not God's will. Fighting against intense, inordinate emotions is not easy, but certainly not impossible, with the enabling grace of God. God's truth can set us free from our sin as we embrace what He has taught us in His Word and as we act on truth rather than on how we feel.

Turning from Idolatrous Emotional Attachments

What we think turns into how we feel and act. When we think (for whatever reason) we cannot live without a person then we will feel intense desires to cling to them. Likely we will then do whatever it takes to try to accomplish keeping them in our life.

Fortunately for Christians caught up in a sinful relationship, there is hope. After Paul gave a dire warning in 1 Corinthians that unrighteous people such as fornicators and homosexuals will not be in God's Kingdom, he gave amazing hope to the Christians to whom he was writing when he said "such *were* some of you!" (1 Cor. 6:11). The grip and power of sin has been broken for the Christian by the Lord Jesus Christ's death on the cross:

> Therefore do not let sin reign in your mortal body so that you obey its lusts, and do not go on presenting the members of your body to sin as instruments of unrighteous-

ness; but present yourselves to God as those alive from the dead, and your members as instruments of righteousness to God. For sin shall not be master over you, for you are not under law but under grace. (Rom. 6:12–14)

Because we have God's command and grace to help us, what are some practical biblical thoughts and actions one can take to break away from idolatrous emotional attachments?

1. *Turn from wrong thinking about the other person to right thinking about God and your responsibility to honor and worship Him.* Instead of thinking, *I can't live without him,* think, *It may be difficult, but there is no one that I can't live without. The Lord will help me and promises to be with me* (see Heb. 13:5). Instead of thinking, *No one will ever love me like he does,* think, *God forbid that anyone would ever love me like this!* True biblical love *"does not rejoice in unrighteousness but rejoices with the truth!"* (see 1 Cor. 13:6). Instead of thinking, *I cannot bear to be alone,* think, *I may be by myself but I am never alone as the Lord is with me. I will praise Him for the help of His presence* (see Ps. 42:5).

2. *Repent of sexual sin and/or sensual thoughts. Express your shame and remorse to God and ask His forgiveness:*

Flee immorality. Every other sin that a man commits is outside the body, but the immoral man sins against his own body. Or do you not know that your body is a temple of the Holy Spirit who is in you, whom you have from God, and that you are not your own? For you have been bought with a price: therefore glorify God in your body. (1 Cor. 6:18–20)

Realize that if you are a Christian, God indwells your body, and you have been redeemed by His blood, as "He Himself bore our sins in His body on the cross, so that we might die to sin and live to righteousness; for by His wounds you were healed" (1 Peter 2:24). Sinful sexual thoughts and actions are shameful. These thoughts and actions are, if you will, "in His face." If you are guilty, take a moment now to pray and express your remorse and sorrow over your sin and then honor God by believing that "if we confess our sins, He is faithful and righteous to forgive us our sins and to cleanse us from all unrighteousness" (1 John 1:9).

3. *Submit yourself to accountability.* Having someone hold you accountable can be embarrassing and humiliating, but it is a key component in breaking away from sinful relationships because God pours out His grace on the humble (James 4:6). Also, Christians are to help each other become as much like the Lord Jesus Christ as possible, and that includes bearing "one another's burdens [in the context of helping a sinning brother], and thereby fulfill the law of Christ" (Gal. 6:2). Often when I am counseling a woman who is struggling to get out of and stay out of a wrong relationship I tell her, "If you have a 'Jim (or whatever the person's name is) attack,' call me and I will help you to think rightly." Accountability is usually critical. Don't let your pride keep you from asking a godly, mature Christian to help bear your burden of sin.

4. *Immerse yourself in the Word of God, meditating on and memorizing Scripture.* The effect of immersing yourself in the Scriptures is simple: "Your Word I have treasured in my heart, That I may not sin against You" (Ps. 119:11). God uses the Scriptures to mature us so that we can "discern good and evil" (Heb. 5:14). God also uses the Scriptures in a supernatural way to judge the thoughts and intentions of your heart (see Heb. 4:12). Christians call this "coming under conviction." This just

means that you feel uneasy or guilty about something you are thinking or doing. Daily time in the Word of God for the child of God is imperative if you are to resist and turn away from sin.

5. *Confront the other person biblically with their sin.* Confronting another person with their sin is usually a very difficult thing to do, especially when the confronter knows that they, too, are guilty (in fact, they may have been the one to entice the other person into the idolatrous relationship!), and they do not want to hurt the other person's feelings. This is understandable, but must be biblically overcome. The Lord Jesus made it clear that we are to "first take the log out of [our] own eye[s], and then [we] will see clearly to take the speck out of [our] brother's eye" (Matt. 7:5). So if you were involved, before you confront the other person, first ask their forgiveness for your part. Then, as the Bible instructs us in Galatians 6:1, gently and with a motive to restore the other person to a right relationship with God and others, confront them. It will not be easy but will be less traumatic if you write out what you want to say and then practice it aloud several times.

6. *Overcome evil with good by setting godly, firm, righteous limits.* "Do not be deceived: 'Bad company corrupts good morals' " (1 Cor. 15:33). To continue in a friendship with someone with whom you have had an idolatrous attachment would make it almost impossible to maintain a chaste life. Instead of risking the possibility of being drawn back into a sinful relationship, realize your freedom in Christ and separate from the other person (see 2 Cor. 6:14–18). Even if the other person claims to be a Christian but persists in their sin, the apostle Paul warns us, "But actually, I wrote to you not to associate with any so-called brother if he is an immoral person . . ." (1 Cor. 5:11). Be crystal clear to the other person concerning the limits you are setting and tell the person who is holding you accountable so they can

make sure that you are maintaining those limits. If the other person is a Christian and is willing to turn from their sin, that person is still potentially a "provision for the flesh" for you (Rom. 13:14). There are simply some risks not worth taking.

7. *Realize that you will never be able to satisfy the other person's idolatrous attachment to you no matter what you do for them.* There is a reason why " 'there is no peace,' says my God, 'for the wicked' " (Isa. 57:21). This is because a person with an idolatrous emotional attachment is longing for and worshiping the wrong god. The love and devotion of another person within a sinful relationship is a lust of the flesh, and it can never be satisfied. If it could be satisfied, then people would easily stop drinking to excess or stop gambling or stop looking at pornography. Since the excitement and enticement of sin can never be satisfied, you must turn from being the person who is trying to satisfy another person's lustful attachment to you. Instead, offer them help through another source.

8. *Provide the other person the name of a contact person and church that would be able to give them the gospel and biblical counsel. If the other person won't take your advice, accept the fact that this is not your problem, but theirs.* Certainly there are two people in an emotionally idolatrous relationship, and as Christians we should care about both of them. Clearly, they should separate from each other, but both need to be offered biblical help through a good local church. None of us can make another person seek help and accountability, but it should be offered nonetheless. As a result, the person who is trying to get help will have done everything they should and must accept the fact that this is all they can do. One word of caution, however: If the other person threatens to harm himself, then the person trying to get them to seek help must contact that person's family and/or the police.

9. *Be passionate and faithful in your worship of God and delight yourself in His ways whether you ever have another friendship or not.* King David faced many trials and tests, including his own sin, but in spite of that David had a whole heart for God (see Acts 13:22). The Psalms show David's heart as his poetry is brimming over with his soul rejoicing in the Lord and exulting in His salvation. Consider a small sampling:

> I would have despaired unless I had believed that I
>   would see the goodness of the LORD
> In the land of the living. (Ps. 27:13–14)

> In You, O LORD, I have taken refuge;
> Let me never be ashamed;
> In Your righteousness deliver me.
> Incline Your ear to me, rescue me quickly;
> Be to me a rock of strength,
> A stronghold to save me.
> For You are my rock and my fortress;
> For Your name's sake You will lead me and guide me.
>   (Ps. 31:1–3)

> O taste and see that the LORD is good;
> How blessed is the man who takes refuge in Him! (Ps.
>   34:8)

> And my soul shall rejoice in the LORD;
> It shall exult in His salvation. (Ps. 35:9)

> Your lovingkindness, O LORD, extends to the heavens,
> Your faithfulness reaches to the skies.
> Your righteousness is like the mountains of God;

Your judgments are like a great deep.
O LORD, You preserve man and beast.
How precious is Your lovingkindness, O God!
And the children of men take refuge in the shadow of
     Your wings.
They drink their fill of the abundance of Your house;
And You give them to drink of the river of Your delights.
For with You is the fountain of life;
In Your light we see light. (Ps. 36:5–9)

Delight yourself in the LORD;
And He will give you the desires of your heart.
Commit your way to the LORD,
Trust also in Him and He will do it.
He will bring forth your righteousness as the light
And your judgment as the noonday. (Ps. 37:4–6)

Righteous friendships are a gift from God but so, too, is contentment—whether you have a special friend or not. The only antidote to loneliness and missing an idolatrous friend is delighting in the Lord and what He is doing in your life. Passionately and faithfully, like David, worship and delight in the Lord. Then you will see how truly good He is.

Conclusion

As mentioned in the beginning of this chapter, idolatrous emotional attachments are those relationships that involve inordinate emotional longings for another person and a belief that you cannot live without them. Like Wendy with her boyfriend or Bob with his homosexual lover, idolatrous relationships often involve sexual immorality. Although it is never easy to turn from an idolatrous attachment, it is possible for people like Wendy and Bob to turn from their sin, and turn to delighting in and worshiping the Lord Jesus Christ as their minds are renewed by Scripture and they seek godly accountability. The power of God is awesome, and He can and does change people for His glory. By God's grace, both Wendy and Bob and perhaps you, too (if you are struggling with an idolatrous emotional attachment), can be like the Christians in Corinth of whom it was written, "Such *were* some of you . . ." (1 Cor. 6:11).

⚬⚬⚬⚬⚬⚬⚬⚬⚬ *Study Questions* ⚬⚬⚬⚬⚬⚬⚬⚬⚬

1. How are idolatrous emotional attachments defined in this chapter?

2. What are some excuses people use to continue in idolatrous relationships?

3. How is someone drawn into an idolatrous relationship?

4. According to Romans 13:14 and Galatians 5:16, how do we overcome our sinful desires?

5. How is it possible to change from a fornicator, homosexual, or adulterer (see 1 Cor. 6:11)?

6. Correct the following wrong thoughts:

    a. *I can't live without him.*

    b. *No one will ever love me like she does.*

    c. *I cannot bear to be alone.*

7. Why is sexual sin so wrong (see 1 Cor. 6:18–20)?

8. Match the following:

God gives grace to the humble.	Hebrews 5:14
Christians are to help each other bear their sin burdens.	Hebrews 4:12
We should be like the psalmist who hid God's Word in his heart.	James 4:6
We must study the Scriptures so that we can discern good and evil.	Psalm 119:11

The Scriptures judge our thoughts   Galatians 6:1–2
and intentions.

11. Write out an example of what you would say when confronting someone with the sin of an idolatrous relationship. (Hint: What should be your motive?)

10. Is it really necessary to set limits (see 1 Cor. 15:33; 5:11; Rom. 13:14)?

11. Instead of trying to satisfy another person's lustful attachment to you, what sort of help should you offer?

12. What actions are needed if one of the people threatens to harm themselves?

13. Instead of delighting in a sinful relationship, whom should we delight in? Read through some of the Psalms and list examples of a psalmist delighting in God.

4

I'm Supposed to Respond *How?*

MANIPULATION

I grew up as an only child—very selfish and very spoiled. As a child, I lived a double life. One of my lives was as a goody two-shoes at school (mainly because I knew the teacher took the bad kids to the principal to be spanked), and the other life was as a spoiled, easily angered, not very grateful kid at home. My parents never disciplined me, and I learned early in my life (my mother said it began when I was a baby) that if I persisted long enough and hard enough that my parents would give in. If having a mother and father who spoiled me wasn't bad enough, I had an aunt and uncle who had no children, and they were like a second set of parents to me. My friends liked to come over to my house because I had so many toys and the largest stack of comic books they had ever seen!

Whether it was as a ten-month-old infant clinging to the side of the crib screaming in anger because I didn't want to be put down or as a teenager begging my parents to let me go somewhere where I knew I really shouldn't be going, I was very skilled at manipulating my parents. Actually I was an expert! An expert that is, at sinning. I was using sinful means to try to have my way, and if I couldn't have my way, I could at least make everyone around me miserable. It would be tempting to blame my behavior (which continued into adulthood and affected other relationships) on my parents and my aunt and uncle, but the Scriptures are clear:

> Yet you say, "Why should the son not bear the punishment for the father's iniquity?" When the son has practiced justice and righteousness and has observed all My statutes and done them, he shall surely live. The person who sins will die. The son will not bear the punishment for the father's iniquity, nor will the father bear the punishment for the son's iniquity; the righteousness of the righteous will be upon himself, and the wickedness of the wicked will be upon himself. (Ezek. 18:19–20)

Since He saved me, God in His mercy has convicted me of my sinful manipulation, and I was able to ask my parents and my aunt and uncle and others to forgive me, and they did. What I was doing is what a lot of people do—using sinful means to try to have my way (and if I couldn't have my way, I could at least upset the person blocking my way). Because sinful manipulation is such a common problem, we will begin with a definition of sinful manipulation and give examples of how it is carried out. Then we will look at how to turn from sinful manipulation to a love for others. Lastly, we will look at how to respond in a God-honoring way when others are trying to manipulate you.

What Is Sinful Manipulation?

Sinful manipulation is using *unbiblical words and/or your countenance to bully another person into letting you have your way. All the while you know that if you cannot have your way, you can at least punish the other person in the process.* Sinful manipulation often escalates as the manipulator presses harder to have her way. Consider some tactics often used in manipulation by studying figure 4.1.

If You Are Guilty

You know you are guilty of sinful manipulation when you don't graciously take "no" for an answer and keep trying to convince the other person to let you have your way. Certainly there

Fig. 4.1 Manipulative Tactics

Manipulating Ploy	Husband and Wife Example
1. Sweet talk	"Sweetheart, you are the best husband in the world and I love you, and I wanted you to know that I think I need a break. Would it be all right if I go to the beach for a week with my girlfriends, and you take care of the children?" (There is nothing wrong with asking, and if a wife's motive is pure she will graciously take "no" for an answer. If her motive is sinful, she will likely proceed to another ploy.)
2. Beg	"*Please, please* let me go. I promise I won't ask again for a long time. *Please say 'yes!'*"
3. Cry	Tears well up in her eyes. "I'm so disappointed. It hurts my feelings that you don't want me to go."
4. Anger	"This makes me so #!*# mad! I want to go!!"
5. Cold Shoulder	She thinks, *I'll show him,* and does not speak to him at all or only speaks in a snippy, cold tone.
6. Accusations	"You don't love me." "You only care about yourself!" "I thought you cared about me." "You're not fair. You get to go to work every day, and I'm stuck at home with these kids. They're driving me crazy."
7. Threats	"If you don't let me go, I'll go anyway and get a baby sitter." "I don't know what I might do if you don't let me go." "I'll leave you and may or may not come back." "If I leave, I'll move away, and you'll never see your kids again." "I'll divorce you." "I'll kill myself."

Manipulating Ploy	Mother and Adult Daughter Example
1. Sweet talk	Mother to daughter, "I am so proud of you and how you take care of your family. I wanted to talk to you about something. Honey, you know my divorce was your dad's fault. He hasn't changed, and I don't want you to let your children see him."
2. Beg	"*Please* don't go visit him. I don't think I could stand it knowing you were spending time with him."
3. Cry	"This really hurts me and upsets me. Please don't go."
4. Anger	"This makes me so angry. It's not right what you are doing. You've got to stop."
5. Cold Shoulder	Talks to her daughter, but is short, aloof, and obviously punishing her. Turns to talk to others in a warm, gracious manner.
6. Accusations	"You're not the daughter I thought you were." "How could you have a relationship with him after all he has done to me?" "I thought you loved me and cared about me." "You were the one person in the world who understood and who cared for me during the divorce." "How can you do this to me after all I've done for you?"
7. Threats	"If you go to visit your dad I will never see you again." "You are ruining my life, and I don't know what I might do."

Manipulating Ploy	Mother and Teenage Son
1. Sweet talk	"Mom, out of all of my friends' moms, you are the best! May I borrow the car tonight to go with my friends to the movies?"
2. Beg	"Mom, *please* let me go. All my friends can go, and I'm the only one who can drive us. If I don't go they won't get to go either. *Please*!"
3. Cry	"Mom, let me take the car. I promise I'll be careful." (Tears in his eyes)
4. Anger	"Why won't you let me go?" (Stomps out of the room and slams his door. Mom can hear him throwing things around in his room.)
5. Cold Shoulder	Refuses to speak to his mom but gives her a cold stare when she tries to talk to him.
6. Accusations	"You're not fair!" "I thought I could depend on you." "You don't love me." "You're being selfish." "You're doing this deliberately to embarrass me in front of my friends."
7. Threats	"I hate you. I can't wait to get away from you." "I will leave here, and you will never see me again." "I'll go anyway, no matter what you say."

may be times when an appeal is appropriate, but if the answer is still "no," then you must see it as God's will for you at the moment. Think about the following Scriptures:

- "Do not be wise in your own eyes; Fear the LORD and turn away from evil." (Prov. 3:7)
- "Put away from you a deceitful mouth And put devious speech far from you." (Prov. 4:24)
- "There is one who speaks rashly like the thrusts of a sword, But the tongue of the wise brings healing." (Prov. 12:18)
- "The heart of the righteous ponders how to answer, But the mouth of the wicked pours out evil things." (Prov. 15:28)
- "A lying tongue hates those it crushes, And a flattering mouth works ruin." (Prov. 26:28)
- "In everything, therefore, treat people the same way you want them to treat you, for this is the Law and the Prophets." (Matt. 7:12)
- "[Love] does not act unbecomingly; it does not seek its own [way]; is not provoked. . . ." (1 Cor. 13:5)
- "Do all things without grumbling or disputing; so that you will prove yourselves to be blameless and innocent, children of God above reproach in the midst of a crooked and perverse generation, among whom you appear as lights in the world, . . ." (Phil. 2:14–15)
- "In everything give thanks; for this is God's will for you in Christ Jesus." (1 Thess. 5:18)

Using unbiblical means such as anger or flattery to try to have your way is wicked. More than likely if you are guilty of this, you may have been guilty of it for a long time, perhaps even as a child. Well, now is the time to grow up and mature in the Lord and stop. Realize that it is all right to ask your grown daughter not to visit her father or to ask your husband to let you take a week-long trip with your girlfriends or for a teenager to ask to borrow the car, *but it is sinful control not to be gracious when told "no."* Before you even ask, plan out what you will think and say if the answer is "no" and see that answer as God's will for you at the moment. Thank the Lord and do not grumble or complain. Ask forgiveness of God for past transgressions, and ask the people whom you have offended to forgive you. Also ask them to hold you accountable to try to stop you if you attempt to unbiblically control them again. If they do point it out, do not counterattack, but ask God to help you see what you are doing wrong, and ask the person confronting you to help you understand. God will help you as He always gives grace to the humble (see James 4:6).

If the Other Person Is Guilty

If someone else is using unbiblical means to try to manipulate you (the world often calls this "verbal abuse"), then you must speak the truth to them in love. So whether it is your grown daughter, your teenage son, your husband, or your friend, they are sinning and acting like a fool. A fool won't take "no" for an answer as "a fool does not delight in understanding, But only in revealing his own mind" (Prov. 18:2). So, I recommend you follow the counsel in Proverbs 26:4–5 for practical advice on how to handle this type situation:[1]

Do not answer a fool according to his folly,
Or you will also be like him. (Prov. 26:4)

A fool answers back in anger or defends himself at length. Fools often counterattack with their own accusations or threats or begging. As tempting as this may be, though, it is returning evil for evil, and instead of just one fool using sinful manipulation, now there are two! So you must learn to:

> Answer a fool as his folly deserves,
> That he not be wise in his own eyes. (Prov. 26:5)

In other words, give the fool an answer that will convict him of his responsibility before God. He may not repent, but at least he will have been told clearly of his responsibility before God. Often the manipulation will stop, but even if it does not, there is only one fool shaking his fist at God instead of two. Also, the person who responds righteously will suffer for righteousness' sake and will honor God. For some examples, let's reconsider figure 4.1, this time adding a third column of how to "answer a fool as his folly deserves" (Prov. 26:5).

Anytime someone uses unbiblical means to try to attain his way, he is sinning. When someone is manipulating you, you are likely to have very unpleasant emotions—fear, confusion, frustration, or guilt. So your emotions will make it difficult for you to respond without sinning (defending yourself, blowing up in anger, sinfully giving in). Therefore, it is important to work diligently to learn how to respond wisely (giving fools the answer they deserve).

If you become confused at any point in the conversation say, "I need to think about what I want to say. I'll be back." Then go somewhere and write down the conversion: "I said. . . ." "he said. . . ." "I said. . . ." "he said. . . ." Once you have the conversation written down, go over it point by point and make sure you are not responding like a fool and that you are giving the fool an answer so that he won't be wise in his own eyes. Then go and say, "Remember when I

Fig. 4.2 Answering a Fool as His Folly Deserves

Manipulating Ploy	Husband and Wife Example	As His Folly Deserves
1. Sweet talk	"Sweetheart, you are the best husband in the world and I love you, and I wanted you to know that I think I need a break. Would it be all right if I go to the beach for a week with my girlfriends, and you take care of the children?"	Husband says, "Honey I wish you could, but this is going to be a really tough week for me at work, and I need you home. Perhaps we can work out something later for a shorter period of time."
2. Beg	"*Please, please* let me go. I promise I won't ask again for a long time. *Please say, 'yes!'*"	Husband says, "Honey I wish I could say 'yes,' but my job to support this family has to come first." (see 1 Cor. 11:3)
3. Cry	Tears well up in her eyes. "I'm so disappointed. It hurts my feelings that you don't want me to go."	Husband says, "Sweetheart, it is your responsibility to graciously take 'no' for an answer and to stay home and not resent it." (see Titus 2:4–5)
4. Anger	In an angry harsh tone of voice, "This makes me so #!*# mad! I want to go!!"	Husband says calmly but clearly, "It's understandable that you are disappointed, but it's not OK to be disappointed and sin in the process. Your responsibility is to put your family first." (see Col. 3:8)
5. Cold Shoulder	She thinks, *I'll show him* and does not speak to him or only speaks in a snippy, cold tone.	Husband says, "Honey, you are being rude and malicious when you act like this. As a Christian, your responsibility is to be 'kind and tender-hearted and forgiving' " (Eph. 4:32).
6. Accusations	"You don't love me." "You only care about yourself!" "I thought you cared about me." "You're not fair. You get to go to work every day and I'm stuck at home with these kids. They're driving me crazy."	Husband says, "Honey, you are using sinful accusations to try to have your way. Instead you should be thinking, *How can I make that week as easy on my husband as possible?* The wife was created 'for the man's sake.' So, my husband's responsibilities at work are more important than my vacation." (see 1 Cor. 11:8–9)
7. Threats	"If you don't let me go, I'll go anyway and get a baby sitter." "I don't know what I might do if you don't let me go." "I'll leave you and may or may not come back." "If I leave, I'll move away and you'll never see your kids again." "I'll divorce you." "I'll kill myself."	Husband says, "Honey, if you do that, you will be sinning, and it will be difficult for me and the children, but God will give us the grace to go through it." (see 1 Cor. 10:13)

Manipulating Ploy	Mother and Adult Daughter Example	As His Folly Deserves
1. Sweet talk	Mother to daughter, "I am so proud of you and how you take care of your family. I wanted to talk to you about something. Honey, you know my divorce was your dad's fault. He hasn't changed, and I don't want you to let your children see him."	Daughter says, "Mom I know that Dad abandoned our family and loved his sin more than he loved his family, but we have decided to visit him to give him a blessing and share the gospel with him." (see 1 Peter 3:9, 15)
2. Beg	"*Please* don't go visit him. I don't think I could stand it knowing you were spending time with him."	Daughter says, "Mom, I know it might be difficult, but God will give you the grace to bear up under this." (see 1 Cor. 10:13)
3. Cry	"This really hurts me and upsets me. You can't do this to me."	Daughter says, "Mom, your responsibility is to give us the freedom in the Lord to reach out to Dad and for you to be glad for Dad that we can visit him. If he doesn't come to know the Lord, his earthly happiness will be all he has." (see James 3:17–18)
4. Anger	"This makes me so angry. It's not right what you are doing. You've got to stop."	Daughter says, "Actually this is the right thing to do. Mom, you are using anger to try to manipulate me so that you can continue to punish Dad for what he has done. Instead, you should pray for his salvation and have mercy on him and be thankful that we are going to see him." (see Matt. 5:7)
5. Cold Shoulder	Talks to her daughter, but is short, aloof, and obviously punishing her. Turns to talk to others in a warm, gracious manner.	"Mom, you're being rude and unkind in order to try to have your way. It's not right. Instead of giving me the cold shoulder, you should be more concerned about my feelings and Dad's salvation than you are focused on yourself." (see Col. 3:12–14)
6. Accusations	"You're not the daughter I thought you were. How could you have a relationship with him after all he has done to me? I thought you loved me and cared about me. You were the one person in the world who understood and who cared for me during the divorce. How can you do this to me after all I've done for you?"	"Mom, listen to yourself. Your responsibility is to graciously give me the freedom to visit Dad, and you should also pray for his salvation. I know that Dad, in a sense, is your enemy, but the Lord Jesus told us to 'love our enemies.' What you are doing is sinful, and you must repent and honor God." (see Matt. 5:43–48)
7. Threats	"If you go to visit your dad I will never see you again. You are ruining my life and I don't know what I might do."	"If you never see me again and if your life is ruined it will be a consequence of your own sin. That would be especially difficult for me, but if you follow through with your threats, God will give me the grace to go through it." (see 1 Cor.10:13)

Manipulating Ploy	Mother and Teenage Son	As His Folly Deserves
1. Sweet talk	"Mom, out of all of my friends' moms, you are the best! May I borrow the car tonight to go with my friends to the movies?"	"No, son. I'm sorry, but I think it would be best if you stayed home tonight and rested for school tomorrow."
2. Beg	"Mom, *please* let me go. All my friends can go, and I'm the only one who can drive us. If I don't go they won't get to go either. *Please!*"	"Son. I'm sorry but this is a wisdom issue, and I think it unwise so you need to stop begging me. How should you have responded when I said, 'No'?" (see Eph. 6:1–2))
3. Cry	"Mom, let me take the car. I promise I'll be careful." (Tears in his eyes)	"Son, your responsibility is graciously to take 'no' for an answer and to repent from demanding your way." (see Prov. 18:2)
4. Anger	"Why won't you let me go?" (Stomps out of the room and slams his door. Mom can hear him throwing things around in his room.)	"Son, you are using anger to try to get your way and to punish me. Instead, you should show love to God by honoring your mother's decision and be grateful to God and to me that you can take the car occasionally." (see Matt. 22:36–39)
5. Cold Shoulder	Refuses to speak to his mom but gives her a cold stare when she tries to talk to him.	"Son, you are still using unbiblical means to manipulate me to get your way. This is not right. What you are doing is sinful, and you are to stop." (see Eph. 6:2)
6. Accusations	"You're not fair! I thought I could depend on you. You don't love me. You're being selfish. You're doing this deliberately to embarrass me in front of my friends."	"Son, you are acting foolish. You say you are a Christian and if you are, you should see my decision as God's will for you. Your responsibility is to graciously and gratefully honor what I say." (see Col. 3:17)
7. Threats	"I hate you. I can't wait to get away from you. I will leave here, and you will never see me again. I'll go anyway, no matter what you say."	"You are being very malicious. If you do those things, it will be difficult for me, but God will give me the grace to endure it, and you will face the consequences of your sin." (see Prov. 18:7)

said . . . ? That's not what I should have said; *this* is what I should have said. . . ." The more you work at thinking factually and biblically instead of responding emotionally, the better you will get at showing love to other people by trying to help them see their responsibility.

All Is Said and Done in Love

When you are engaged in a verbal battle with a bully, remember that "the anger of man does not achieve the righteousness of

God" (James 1:20). If the shoe were on the other foot and you were the one acting like a fool, think about how you would want someone to reprove you. Speak in a kind, gentle tone of voice because "love is patient, love is kind" (1 Cor. 13:4). Ask the Lord to help you and, if necessary, excuse yourself to go pray and practice aloud what you want to say. Have as your heart's desire to be like the Lord Jesus Christ, who never spoke in sinful, unbridled anger or foolish, proud defense of Himself. He always perfectly showed love for God and for others even when (and especially when) they were sinning. "Do nothing from selfishness or empty conceit, but with humility of mind regard one another as more important than yourselves" (Phil. 2:3). So, learn to speak the truth in love and be assured that regardless of how the sinful manipulator sins you can "keep a good conscience so that in the thing in which you are slandered, those who revile your good behavior in Christ will be put to shame. For it is better, if God should will it so, that you suffer for doing what is right rather than for doing what is wrong" (1 Peter 3:16–17).

Conclusion

Sinful manipulation is using your words and/or countenance to bully or persuade another person to let you have your way. If you cannot have your way, you can at least punish the other person in the process. It is sin, but by God's grace it can be overcome. Whether you or someone else is guilty of manipulation, it is wrong, and shows a lack of love toward God and the other person. If you are the guilty one, ask forgiveness of God and others and seek accountability. Humbly listen to reproof and learn from it. If the other person is guilty, work diligently to understand and implement in your speech how to not answer like a fool but, instead, give the fool the answer he deserves. Don't be like the angry, selfish, spoiled brat that I was. Receive a "no" answer as God's will for you at the moment and graciously honor God.

❧❧❧❧❧❧ *Study Questions* ❧❧❧❧❧❧

1. How is sinful manipulation defined in this chapter?

2. List the seven typical manipulative ploys in their usual order. Think of an example of each one or adapt one of the examples in this chapter.

3. How can you know if you are guilty of sinful manipulation?

4. Instead of responding sinfully, how should you (or others) respond? List several Scriptures.

5. According to Proverbs 18:2, what is a person acting like when she won't take "no" for an answer?

6. What are some foolish ways you might respond back to a fool (see Prov. 26:4)?

7. What kind of answer should you give to a fool (see Prov. 26:5)?

8. For the following example, write out an "as her folly deserves" reply:

Manipulating Ploy	Two Adult Girlfriends	As Her Folly Deserves
1. Sweet Talk	Jan says, "Sue, I would like you to go shopping with me next Saturday. It would be fun and we could invite Janet to meet us for lunch."	Sue says, "That does sound like fun but I promised my husband I would stay home and get caught up on my house work. Maybe next time."
2. Beg	"Sue, please go. It won't be any fun if you don't go. I'm sure your husband would want you to have a break from the house."	
3. Cry	"I'm so disappointed. It hurts my feelings that you don't want to go." (Tears in her eyes)	
4. Anger	"Well, maybe next time!" (In a harsh, sarcastic tone of voice)	

5. Cold Shoulder	Sue calls Jan on the phone the next day, and Jan is cool, aloof, and abrupt in her answers.
6. Accusations	Jan says, "I thought you were my friend. After all I have done for you, it seems like you could do this one little thing. You are letting your husband bully you."
7. Threats	"Well, I guess I'll just have to find a new friend. Word will get out at church that you have hurt me. Some Christian you are."

9. What should you do if at any time in the conversation you become confused?

5

What Difference Does It Make *What* He Intended?

HURT FEELINGS

When I was a child growing up I cannot remember either of my parents ever saying, "That hurt my feelings!" I can remember them saying to me, "You're being selfish" or "That's not right." Because they never talked about their feelings being hurt, I guess I never learned to think in terms of *my hurt feelings*. Since I have become an adult, however, there have been occasions when someone has said or done something that has caused me to think, *My feelings are hurt!* Also, since becoming a biblical counselor, I have counseled many women who have told me how their feelings have been hurt, and more often than not, I could certainly understand why. Let's consider the following examples:

- "How could he have lied about me like that? That hurt my feelings."
- "She wouldn't let me help her. That hurt my feelings."
- "He deliberately embarrassed me in front of my friends. That hurt my feelings."

73

- "My Sunday school teacher called on me to pray. She should have known that makes me uncomfortable. That hurt my feelings."
- "Why did my girlfriends not invite me to the luncheon? That hurt my feelings."
- "The lady introducing me mispronounced my name. Everyone snickered. That hurt my feelings."
- "I would never have treated her the way she treated me. That hurt my feelings."
- "He got angry when I simply asked a question. That hurt my feelings."
- "The committee never seems to like my ideas. I'm not going back. They hurt my feelings."
- "He said he was teasing me, but it made me feel uncomfortable. My feelings are hurt."
- "Who does he think he is to tell me what I'm doing wrong? He's not so perfect! He hurt my feelings."
- "My father drank and neglected our family. He rejected me, and my feelings are hurt."
- "My husband left me for another woman. That hurt my feelings."
- "The elders didn't like my suggestion for the order of the service at church. I wish I had never suggested it. They hurt my feelings."

From these examples we can see that there are a variety of ways that someone can have their feelings hurt. The purpose of this chapter is to consider what *are* hurt feelings, what *causes* hurt feelings, and what does the Bible *teach* us about how to overcome hurt feelings. Let's begin by defining hurt feelings.

Just What Are Hurt Feelings?

Feelings are emotions, and emotions occur after we think something. For example, if I think, *I just know this plane is going to crash!* then I will feel anxious. If I think, *I can't believe he did that to me. That makes me so angry!* I will feel frustrated. If I think, *He did that deliberately to make me look like a fool.* I will feel hurt.

Webster's Dictionary defines emotional hurt as "mental distress or anguish."[1] The emotional pain that we experience when our feelings are hurt can vary in degree from slight to overwhelming. The pain from hurt feelings can be so great that you cannot sleep because of thinking of how another person has hurt you. The hurt may also be so great that the pain returns fifty years later when reminded of the long ago "hurt." This kind of emotional pain can be incapacitating or at the least very unsettling and unpleasant. To really understand what hurt feelings are and what to do about them, we need to consider what the Scriptures teach us. Let's begin with the word *hurt.*

When you look the word *hurt* up in the Bible, you find several references. Some refer to physical hurt and some refer to emotional hurt. For the purposes of this study, we will look at two that refer to emotional hurt.

The slain will fall among you, and you will know that I am the LORD.

However, I will leave a remnant, for you will have those who escaped the sword among the nations when you are scattered among the countries. Then those of you who escape will remember Me among the nations to which they will be carried captive, how I have been *hurt* by their adulterous hearts which turned away from

Me, and by their eyes which played the harlot after their idols; and they will loathe themselves in their own sight for the evils which they have committed, for all their abominations. (Ezek. 6:7–9)

There were times when the children of Israel, in spite of all the revelation they had from God, turned from worship of Him to worship of idols. In the Old Testament, God refers to Himself as Israel's husband. So like an unfaithful wife sinning against her husband, Israel committed (spiritual) adultery. This, of course, hurt God. The Hebrew word for *hurt* here means "disgrace, humiliation, shame, or reproach."[2] The people's idolatry was a shameful, grievous reproach on God, especially after all He had done for them:

In the New Testament we see a different kind of hurt. "For if because of food your brother is *hurt*, you are no longer walking according to love. Do not destroy with your food him for whom Christ died" (Rom. 14:15).

In this passage, the Greek word for *hurt* means to "cause sorrow, grief, or to be made sorrowful."[3] During the early days of the New Testament church, idolatry was rampant, and one aspect of idol worship was animal sacrifices. Often some of the meat sacrificed to these idols was then sold in the open market place. Many of the new Christians had previously been idolaters, so for them the very thought of eating meat that had been sacrificed to an idol was sickening and considered sinful. Paul explained to them in Romans 14 that sacrificing meat to an idol did not make the meat unclean. However, for the sake of those who thought it was unclean (and were new Christians), the more mature Christians should abstain from eating such meat. Otherwise, they would cause the new Christians unnecessary grief or sorrow. In other words, it would hurt them.

We have seen at least one way to hurt people and also to hurt God Himself. Whether the hurt caused grief, harm, humiliation, or shame, the biblical examples we have looked at happened because of sin. Hurts due to sin are usually intentional, but there is another kind of hurt that is unintentional; *in other words, no harm is intended but it is perceived otherwise.* Now let's consider what to do with hurts, whether intentional or unintentional.

Overcoming Intentional Hurts

Intentional hurts are sinful. They may be in the form of slander, name-calling, malicious comments and acts, or cruel threats. Whatever the form, you can overcome them only by responding righteously, not by adding additional wickedness. Several basic biblical principles give us practical guidance about this subject:

1. *Show love to God and the person sinning against you.*

"Teacher, which is the great commandment in the Law?" And He said to him, " 'YOU SHALL LOVE THE LORD YOUR GOD WITH ALL YOUR HEART, AND WITH ALL YOUR SOUL, AND WITH ALL YOUR MIND.' This is the great and foremost commandment. The second is like it, 'YOU SHALL LOVE YOUR NEIGHBOR AS YOURSELF.' " (Matt. 22:36–39; see also 1 John 4:20–21)

The way to show love to God is to obey His Word. Unlike the slave who would not forgive his fellow slave a small debt even though his master had forgiven him a huge debt, we are to love the person sinning against us. Our initial thought should be, *Lord, knowing that I have done worse sin than this and You have forgiven me, how can I help this person? Help me not to dwell on the hurt, but to honor You.* Even in the worst case where another person is maliciously verbally attacking you or talking about you behind your back, you *can* show love to God and to that person. You show love to God by obeying His Word, and you show love to the other person by being kind, patient, and not playing over and over in your mind what he or she has done. As a Christian you will be vindicated either now or in eternity, and you can cling to the promise that, "If you are reviled for the name of Christ, you are blessed, because the Spirit of glory and of God rests on you" (1 Peter 4:14).

2. *Thank God for the test.*

Always giving thanks for all things in the name of our Lord Jesus Christ to God, even the Father. (Eph. 5:20)

It will help you greatly to look at life from an eternal perspective. What is God doing? What does He want me to learn from this test? Scripture commands me to, "in everything give thanks; for this is God's will for you in Christ Jesus" (1 Thess. 5:18). Certainly it is not pleasant to be sinned against, but it should be your joy to be tried and tested by God because you know that He is molding your character into Christlikeness. So, when thinking of the other person's sin against you, thank God for what He is trying to teach you.

3. *Overcome evil with good.*

Do not be overcome by evil, but overcome evil with good. (Rom. 12:21)

In the Atlanta interstate system there are entrance ramps that appear to go completely opposite of the direction you want to go. You enter those ramps by faith in the signs, certainly not by sight. Once on the ramp you begin to see the almost 360-degree circle that will ultimately take you in the direction you desire. Overcoming evil with good is like those expressway ramps. Our natural tendency is to fight back against evil with more evil. If someone is angry at us, we lash back at them. If they are mean to us, we are mean to them or, at the least, we brood about it in our hearts. But like entering the expressway ramp by faith, we return good for evil by faith. God's command is clear: "Do not be overcome by evil, but overcome evil with good." You do not have to feel like it, you do not have to desire it, and the other person does not have to deserve it, but you do have to respond righteously.

4. Give a blessing instead.

Not returning evil for evil or insult for insult, but giving a blessing instead; for you were called for the very purpose that you might inherit a blessing. (1 Peter 3:9)

The apostle Peter makes it clear that we are not to return evil for evil but give a blessing instead. Think about the person who has hurt you; think of something practical that you can do for him that would bless him. Then do it. If you cannot think of anything, ask God to help you.

5. Pray for those who mistreat you.

Bless those who curse you, pray for those who mistreat you. (Luke 6:28)

In the context of the Sermon on the Mount when the Lord Jesus says, "Pray for those who mistreat you," I do not think that He meant for you to pray, "Lord, rain down fire and brimstone

on her!" or "Kill him!" or "Show her what it's like!" I think He
meant for you to pray for their well being, their repentance, and
that they will give God glory.

6. *Speak the truth in love.*

But speaking the truth in love, we are to grow up in all
aspects into Him who is the head, even Christ. (Eph.
4:15)

Speaking the truth in love is often difficult for us because
of our sinful hearts. It seems to be especially difficult when we
are tired or caught off guard. These are times when it is very
important to be slow to speak (James 1:19). Perhaps you may
even need to say, "I'm not sure how to answer you but I will get
back with you" (see Prov. 15:28). Then pray about it, and think
about it, and *do* get back with them. Speaking the truth in love
involves not only telling the truth but also using a kind tone of
voice because "love is kind" (1 Cor. 13:4).

7. *Lovingly confront the person who is sinning against you.*

Brethren, even if anyone is caught in any trespass, you
who are spiritual, restore such a one in a spirit of gentle-
ness; each one looking to yourself, so that you too will
not be tempted. (Gal. 6:1)

According to this, *you* are to confront the other person's sin
with a motive to restore them to a right relationship with God
and others. Do this gently just as you would want to be confronted if you were doing something wrong. Just this week I heard of
someone who thinks that a reproof is cruel. Their belief is that
you simply pray for a person who is sinning and God will take
care of it. Not only is reproof not cruel (if done in love), but it is

also a mark of Christian maturity when you try to help someone who is in sin. Love "does not rejoice in unrighteousness, but rejoices with the truth" (1 Cor. 13:6). You may avoid a confrontation because you are thinking, *It won't do any good. He will just be more angry with me.* Instead, your thinking needs to change to, *Whether it does any good or not, I am going to obey God and show love to this person whether he perceives the reproof correctly or not. If he does react in sinful pride and anger, it will be difficult for me, but God will be glorified and I will be suffering for doing what is right.*

8. *Bring other witnesses into the situation if necessary.*

> If your brother sins, go and show him his fault in private; if he listens to you, you have won your brother. But if he does not listen to you, take one or two more with you, so that BY THE MOUTH OF TWO OR THREE WITNESSES EVERY FACT MAY BE CONFIRMED. If he refuses to listen to them, tell it to the church; and if he refuses to listen even to the church, let him be to you as a Gentile and a tax collector. Truly I say to you, whatever you bind on earth shall have been bound in heaven; and whatever you loose on earth shall have been loosed in heaven. (Matt. 18:15–18)

The Lord Jesus gave us clear step-by-step instructions about what to do when a fellow believer is sinning. First, you go to them privately. If he repents, that is the end of the matter. If he does not repent, you take two or more witnesses with you. Be an accurate and truthful witness. Don't exaggerate or underplay the truth. Simply speak the truth in a kind way. If, then, he does not repent, take it to the church. Normally this means that you go to the elders in your church, and they will investigate the matter and decide whether to proceed with church discipline.[4]

Our Lord endured much suffering due to the intentional sin of others. We also participate (as Paul wrote) to a tiny degree in the "fellowship of His sufferings" when by His grace we respond righteously (see Phil. 3:10). He understands and will help us. It is a privilege to suffer for the Lord's sake and to be used for His glory.

Now that we have considered how to biblically respond to intentional hurts, let's turn our attention to hurts that are unintentional.

Overcoming Unintentional Hurts

Unintentional hurts are sinful on the part of the person perceiving something as hurtful. Often the person perceiving something as hurtful is overly sensitive, shy, proud, and self-absorbed. Whatever form their sin tends to take, they are to have a righteous, humble response to others.

Instead of being offended and hurt, we must learn to give others the benefit of the doubt. In Philippians 4:8 we are told to think true and lovely thoughts. True thoughts face reality. Lovely thoughts assume the best about the other person unless you can prove otherwise. Therefore, unless it is *crystal clear* that what the other person said or did was intended to hurt you, you must give them the benefit of the doubt. When you give someone the benefit of the doubt, you also show them love, because "love believes all things" (1 Cor. 13:7).

Do not judge people's motives. Judging other's motives and assuming they mean to hurt you is probably the single most common reason why people are overly sensitive and too easily hurt. Since we do not have omniscient understanding (even if we think we are especially perceptive), only our Lord Jesus will be able to rightly "disclose the motives of men's hearts" (1 Cor. 4:5). And until He does, we are forbidden to do so.

We must be willing to feel uncomfortable in order to help others feel comfortable. It is never pleasant to feel uncomfortable, but it is a mark of maturity when your concern is greater for another person's feelings than your own. Paul instructs us to "do nothing from selfishness or empty conceit, but with humility of mind regard one another as more important than yourselves . . ." (Phil. 2:3). So, when you're uncomfortable, tell yourself this: "I feel uncomfortable, but I am going to show love to her. If I have to continue to feel uncomfortable, I'll just have to feel this way."

Now that we have explained some practical, biblical principles on how to respond to a hurt, let's revisit the list at the beginning of this chapter and see how to respond by giving God glory and showing love to the other person instead of thinking in terms of "my hurt feelings" (see Fig. 5.1).

Conclusion

When people hurt your feelings, it may be that they intentionally and sinfully try to harm you. If that is the case, your responsibility is to use biblical resources to, by God's grace, overcome evil with good (Rom. 12:21). If the hurt was not intentional, but your response was sinful, you must repent. Instead of being overly sensitive as you focus on yourself, you must be humble and focus on true and lovely thoughts about the other person.

My parents were right to teach me not to think in terms of *my hurt feelings*. Instead, all of us should think in terms of *loving God and loving others*.

Fig. 5.1 Glorifying God and Showing Love

The Hurt	Biblical Response: Glorifying God and Showing Love
"How could he have lied about me like that? That hurts my feelings."	"What he said is not true. I must go to him (giving him the benefit of the doubt), tell him what I heard that he said, and ask him about it. If he becomes defensive, I'll tell him he must stop slandering me, and, as a Christian, he must give God glory and repent. If he has a reasonable explanation or if he heard bad information somewhere else, I will ask him to go back and straighten it out. Then I will trust God because I have done everything appropriate for me to do."
"She wouldn't let me help her. That hurt my feelings."	"I offered to help, and she has the freedom in the Lord not to accept my help. I'll find something else to do."
"He deliberately embarrassed me in front of my friends. That hurt my feelings."	"What he said or did was unkind. He was sinning. I will speak to him later in private about his unkind words and exhort him to be kind and honor God with his words."
"My Sunday school teacher called on me to pray. She should have known that makes me uncomfortable. That hurt my feelings."	"There really is no way that my Sunday school teacher could have known that praying in front of others would make me uncomfortable. Praying was good for me, or the Lord wouldn't have permitted it. I need to practice praying aloud at home, and then it won't feel so awkward in public."
"Why did my girlfriends not invite me to the luncheon? That hurt my feelings."	"Perhaps they thought I wouldn't be able to attend or perhaps they needed to talk about something that was personal and had nothing to do with me. I'll wait a while and invite them to lunch."
"The lady introducing me mispronounced my name. Everyone snickered. That hurt my feelings."	"Anyone can make a mistake, and it was funny. I need to not be so sinfully proud. Instead, I should be more concerned about making her comfortable than I am about myself."
"I would never have treated her the way she treated me. That hurt my feelings."	"I am perfectly capable of sinning worse than she sinned. I will give her a blessing and try to help her."
"He got angry when I simply asked a question. That hurt my feelings."	"He was sinning and not showing love when he got angry. Lord, what should I say in response that will convict him to be patient, honor You, and show love to others?"
"The committee never seems to like my ideas. I'm not going back. They hurt my feelings."	"They don't have to like my ideas. These decisions are to be made by the majority of the committee. I must graciously put up with differences of opinion, realizing that there are often many ways to accomplish a task."
"He said he was teasing me, but it made me feel uncomfortable. My feelings are hurt."	"I will ask my friend, who was also there, if she thinks I'm being overly sensitive (and therefore sinfully proud). If she thinks his teasing was 'hostile' then I will confront him with his sin. If she thinks his teasing was good natured, then I will ask God to make me humble."
"Who does he think he is to tell me what I'm doing wrong? He's not so perfect! He hurt my feelings."	"He may be right. I need to at least consider what he said and tell him I will think about it and ask the Lord to show me my sin."

The Hurt	Biblical Response: Glorifying God and Showing Love
"My father drank and neglected our family. He rejected me, and my feelings are hurt."	"My father was a drunkard and did neglect his family. He was sinning, but it would not have mattered who his family was because he was not deliberately trying to hurt me. I must forgive him and seek opportunities to give him the gospel and offer him the hope of Christ."
"My husband left me for another woman. That hurt my feelings."	"What he did was very wicked and wrong, but God is good and has a purpose in this for me. I will pray for my husband's salvation and seek ways to honor God in this special trial."
"The elders didn't like my suggestion for the order of the service at church. I wish I had never suggested it. They hurt my feelings."	"It's all right if they don't like my suggestion. They have the authority to accept or reject my idea. It is not a sin issue. At least they didn't say it was a dumb idea!"

Study Questions

1. List three examples of times when your feelings were hurt.

2. Where do hurt feelings come from?

3. According to Ezekiel 6:7–9, how did the children of Israel hurt God?

4. How might exercising our freedoms in the Lord hurt a weaker brother (see Rom. 14:15)?

5. List the eight biblical principles to overcome an intentional hurt. Think of a personal example for each one.

6. What is an "unintentional hurt"?

7. Often, what sins are involved when you experience unintentional hurts?

8. Instead of assuming the worst about another person's motives, what should you assume? Use Scripture to back up your answer.

9. Go back to the three examples you listed in question 1 and write out a biblical response.

PART TWO

∞

Biblical Solutions for Problems with Ourselves

∞

"*But* I say, walk by the Spirit, and you will not carry out the desire of the flesh. For the flesh sets its desire against the Spirit, and the Spirit against the flesh; for these are in opposition to one another, so that you may not do the things that you please."
Galatians 5:16–17

6

Who Is the Fairest of Them All?

VANITY

"Mirror, mirror on the wall who's the fairest of them all? Well, obviously it is not you or me, and we are miserable!" The fact is that many women are utterly miserable because of the way they look. Their desire to be beautiful is so great that they will even succumb to life-threatening makeovers so that they will feel better about themselves. The love of beauty is nothing new— legend has it that a beautiful Greek youth named Narcissus pined away for love of his own image. He stared into a pool of water looking at his beauty for so long that he turned into a narcissus flower (a daffodil).

We have our own versions of Narcissus today. I read about a woman who spent her entire inheritance on extreme plastic surgery because she wanted to look like a Barbie doll. Well, you and I might not do something so painfully foolish, but we might get depressed and feel sorry for ourselves if we do not look a certain way or wear a certain dress size. We find ourselves comparing our looks to the looks of other women everywhere we go. When we do that, we are vain. We are, like Narcissus, pining away for the love of beauty.

In this chapter we will define vanity, learn Scripture's emphasis on true beauty, see the biblical view of a vain woman, and study what the Scriptures warn us about vanity. Let's begin with the definition of vanity.

What Is Vanity?

Vanity is something that is "empty, futile, vain, or worthless. Vanity (in the sense of the love of beauty) is an inflated pride in one's appearance."[1] It is a universal problem, but it especially plagues women. The Jewish women during Isaiah's time offer a vivid example of vain women.[2] They were living examples of how decadent their society had become. Along with the men, they had become like the pagan and carnal societies around them. God was about to severely judge their sin when He sent Isaiah, the prophet, to warn them.

Isaiah warned the Jewish people that the nation of Judah (the southern part of Israel) would be taken into slavery by King Nebuchadnezzar of Babylon. They had turned from serving the one, true God to serving other gods. One of these gods was the god of beauty:

> Moreover, the LORD said, "Because the daughters of
>   Zion are proud
> And walk with heads held high and seductive eyes,
> And go along with mincing steps
> And tinkle the bangles on their feet,
> Therefore the Lord will afflict the scalp of the daughters
>   of Zion with scabs,
> And the LORD will make their foreheads bare." (Isa.
>   3:16–17)

These women were proud and sensual. Don't you think they were quite a sight with their prissy little steps and noisy little bells on their feet to attract attention? The efforts they took to look beautiful were extreme. God's judgment was directly aimed at their vanity:

> In that day the Lord will take away the beauty of their anklets, headbands, crescent ornaments, dangling earrings, bracelets, veils, headdresses, ankle chains, sashes, perfume boxes, amulets, finger rings, nose rings, festal robes, outer tunics, cloaks, money purses, hand mirrors, undergarments, turbans and veils.

> > Now it will come about that instead of sweet perfume there will be putrefaction;
> > Instead of a belt, a rope [to take them off as slaves];
> > Instead of well-set hair, a plucked-out scalp;
> > Instead of fine clothes, a donning of sackcloth;
> > And branding instead of beauty. (Isa. 3:18–24)

This is not a pretty picture; neither is it pretty to God when we spend inordinate amounts of time and money to be beautiful and to call attention to ourselves. To become discerning about vanity in yourself, consider the signs listed in figure 6.1.

Now that we have seen some of the signs of vanity, let's turn to what the Scriptures teach us.

Scripture's Emphasis on True Beauty

> Charm is deceitful and beauty is vain,
> But a woman who fears the LORD, she shall be praised.
> (Prov. 31:30)

Fig. 6.1 Discerning Vanity in Yourself

Sign of Vanity	Particular Example
Are overly concerned about how you look.	• You find yourself closely inspecting every little spot and wrinkle. • You frequently wonder what other people are thinking and saying about how you look. • If you would even dare to venture out of the house on a bad hair/puffy eyes day, you would be very self-conscious and uncomfortable.
Are unable to graciously receive compliments.	• Instead of gratefully enjoying a compliment, you become embarrassed or angry. • Since you do not feel pretty or think you look nice, you are upset that someone would call attention to you.
Feel depressed or anxious because you are "fat."	• Instead of gratefully and joyously serving the Lord each and every day, you are miserable because of your weight.
Are on an unhealthy quest for thinness.	• You sinfully abuse your body through eating disorders such as bulimia, anorexia, fad diets, or extreme exercise.
Overspend on clothes, hair, and makeup.	• You are out of balance in how much you spend on your clothes, hair, and makeup compared to what you give to the Lord or spend on others. • Your priority is how you look, not giving God glory.
Compare yourself to others and how they look.	• You look at the other women in church and think, *I look better than she does today* or *I look awful today. Look at her—she's lost so much weight. I look old and ugly.*
Say things to elicit compliments from others.	• In order to receive the compliments you long for, you ask, "How do I look?" • You put yourself down regarding your looks hoping that others will disagree with you.
Refuse to have sex with your husband because: "I feel ugly" or "I feel fat."	• You are more concerned about how you look and feel than you are concerned about showing love to your husband. • You are selfish by refusing to have sex with your husband.
Apologize for how you look.	• Usually an apology about your looks is the first statement out of your mouth when you run into someone you know. • Even though you may not say anything, you feel very self-conscious about how you look.

Something that is vain is futile, worthless, useless, amounts to nothing, and is a mere breath. Obviously, pursuing vanity is a colossal waste of time! Ultimately anyone over the age of 50 will tell you that it is a losing battle. What *is* going to be important in the eternal long run is how much we loved the Lord. Since we have only so much time on this earth, what do we want to see when we look back over our lives? Sitting in front of a mirror and pining away is a shameful waste of time. We clearly see the depth of futility when we compare a vain woman to a woman who "fears the Lord!"

The New Testament describes the adornment of a truly beautiful woman as one who is adorned with modest and discrete clothing, good works, and a "gentle and quiet spirit."

> Likewise, I want women to adorn themselves with *proper clothing*, modestly and discreetly, not with braided hair and gold or pearls or costly garments, but rather by means of *good works*, as is proper for women making a claim to godliness. (1 Tim. 2:9–10)

> Your adornment must not be merely external — braiding the hair, and wearing gold jewelry, or putting on dresses; but let it be the hidden person of the heart, with the imperishable quality of a *gentle and quiet spirit*, which is precious in the sight of God. (1 Peter 3:3–4)

First, a woman's clothing is to be modest and discrete. Everywhere I go it seems that I cannot help but notice the tightness of clothing styles. The resulting immodesty is shameful and sexually enticing to men. If a woman does not know how her dress affects men, then she is naive. However, if she does know and continues to dress in a provocative way, then it could be she is a sensual woman in her heart.

The women in Paul's day were ostentatious in their dress and manner. You may have seen their pictures or statues with massive bee hive hairdos entwined with braids and gold and pearls. They thought they were lovely, but we think they were ridiculous. Regardless of whether we are talking about over-the-top bee hives or nearly naked women with skin-tight tops and pants, the biblical principle remains the same. Godly adornment requires proper clothing that is modest and discrete. Often I have women ask me for guidelines about how tight something can be or how short or low cut is acceptable? And my answer is, "If you have to ask, then most likely it is not modest." It is very tempting to make up rules, but outward rules do not make a person godly. What does make you godly is God working in your heart. A woman who loves the Lord will have a heart to be modest with her dress in order to not cause men to be tempted to lust.

A second emphasis for a woman who claims to be godly is that her beauty is to be seen in her good works. When I think of a woman who is known for her good works, I think about my friend Patty Thorn. She is always doing something for someone behind the scenes, and often that includes me or my family. She looks for ways to serve. She will cook and clean, or visit and read the Bible and pray for an invalid. She teaches the little girls in her Sunday school class to be servants when she takes them to nursing homes and assisted living homes to visit patients. She helps the girls prepare gifts and practice songs to sing. Patty spreads joy wherever she goes and is eager to tell others about the Lord. Everyone who knows Patty loves her because she shows exemplary godliness through her good works. She is a godly woman, and truly beautiful.

The third biblical emphasis for true beauty in a woman is that she should have a gentle and quiet spirit. This does not mean that she whispers when she talks. It does mean that she is not given to anger or fear, and that she accepts God's dealings with her as good. She is grateful to God and perceives what He is doing as good even if her outward beauty is fading (or was never there in the first place).

When I think about a woman with a gentle and quiet spirit, I think about my mother. As she grew older and her outward beauty faded, I never heard her complain. She was never overly concerned about how she looked, and told me that no matter how old she was, she still felt like the same person on the inside. While my mother was not known for her exceptional beauty, she was known for being patient and kind. This is the kind of Christian woman that we should all aspire to be because she is "precious in the sight of God" (1 Peter 3:4).

The Biblical View of a Vain Woman

We have seen Scripture's emphasis on true beauty, now let's think about how the world views vanity contrasted with the Scriptural view. Your doctor would diagnose you with a *body image problem*, or perhaps your psychologist would say you must have experienced *hurts from childhood* so that your *security and significance* needs were not met. These views are vividly contrasted in Scripture. Consider Scripture's view of a vain woman:

She is not grateful.

> Rejoice always; pray without ceasing; in everything give thanks; for this is God's will for you in Christ Jesus. (1 Thess. 5:16–18)

She is not content.

> But godliness actually is a means of great gain when accompanied by contentment. (1 Tim. 6:6)

She thinks too highly of herself.

> For through the grace given to me I say to everyone among you not to think more highly of himself than he ought to think; but to think so as to have sound judgment, as God has allotted to each a measure of faith. (Rom. 12:3)

She has a lust for beauty.

> But each one is tempted when he is carried away and enticed by his own lust. Then when lust has conceived, it gives birth to sin; and when sin is accomplished, it brings forth death. (James 1:14–15)

She is not motivated by love for God or others, but by the love of self and others' approval.

> Do not love the world nor the things in the world. If anyone loves the world, the love of the Father is not in him. For all that is in the world, the lust of the flesh and the lust of the eyes and the boastful pride of life, is not from the Father, but is from the world. The world is passing away, and also its lusts; but the one who does the will of God lives forever. (1 John 2:15–17)

Instead of being jealous of other women who are more beautiful, we should be glad for them. This is one way we can show love by being "not jealous" (1 Cor. 13:4). In addition, we can learn to accept compliments graciously. Believe that other people are sincere, and therefore do not judge their motives. It is rude not to receive a compliment graciously because love "does not act unbecomingly" (1 Cor. 13:5). Instead, think a "lovely" thought about the other person, believing she is sincere (Phil. 4:8). If you feel uncomfortable and embarrassed, confess your sin of pride to God and say, "Thank you."

Early one morning I came into our kitchen to get a cup of coffee and found a friend who was visiting already up and in the kitchen. He said to me, "You look especially nice today." I was surprised with what he said because I had just gotten out of the bed and thrown my robe on to go to the kitchen. Even though I didn't feel like his compliment could possibly be true, I said, "Thank you." It was only later when I looked in a mirror that I figured out he had been teasing me. I had a rather large amount of mascara smudged under both eyes and I looked like a raccoon! So, whether you really look like a raccoon or not, assume others' compliments are sincere and be gracious. If you know they were teasing you, laugh at yourself!

Remind yourself that true beauty lies on the inside not the outside. Abraham's wife, Sarah, is a good example. Scripture tells us that she was beautiful. Even late in her life (and we know she was really old!) she adorned herself by being submissive and respectful to her husband. Being outwardly beautiful did not earn her the honor of being called a holy woman, but being godly on the inside made her an example for all of us to follow:

> For in this way in former times the holy women also, who hoped in God, used to adorn themselves, being submissive to their own husbands; just as Sarah obeyed Abraham, calling him lord, and you have

become her children if you do what is right without
being frightened by any fear. (1 Peter 3:5–6)

Our most precious example of true beauty is that of our triune God. We know that the Lord Jesus was not a handsome man
and that He had "no stately form or majesty that we should look
upon Him, nor appearance that we should be attracted to Him"
(Isa. 53:2). Yet David wrote of the "beauty of [His] holiness" (Ps.
29:2 KJV). David also desired to see the Lord in His beauty and
described his desire in Psalm 27:

> One thing I have asked from the LORD, that I shall seek:
> That I may dwell in the house of the LORD all the days
>   of my life,
> To behold the beauty of the LORD
> And to meditate in His temple. (Ps. 27:4)

Scriptural Warnings Regarding Vanity

Beauty is vain. It is a depressing pursuit, ultimately hopeless and
empty:

> Charm is deceitful and beauty is vain,
> But a woman who fears the LORD, she shall be praised.
>   (Prov. 31:30)

Beauty is one of the ways the adulteress draws her prey:

> To keep you from the evil woman,
> From the smooth tongue of the adulteress.
> Do not desire her beauty in your heart,
> Nor let her capture you with her eyelids. (Prov. 6:24–25)

Jerusalem trusted in the beauty God had bestowed on her and she played the (spiritual) harlot:

> "Then your fame went forth among the nations on account of your beauty, for it was perfect because of My splendor which I bestowed on you," declares the Lord GOD. "But you trusted in your beauty and played the harlot because of your fame, and you poured out your harlotries on every passer-by who might be willing." (Ezek. 1 6:14–15)

Satan's heart was lifted up because of his beauty:

> "You were the anointed cherub who covers,
> And I [God] placed you there.
> You were on the holy mountain of God. . . .
> You were blameless in your ways
> From the day you were created
> Until unrighteousness was found in you. . . .
> Your heart was lifted up because of your beauty;
> You corrupted your wisdom by reason of your splendor."
> (Ezek. 28:14–15, 17)

Outward beauty without inner beauty is a monstrosity:

> As a ring of gold in a swine's snout
> so is a beautiful woman who lacks discretion. (Prov. 11:22)

A Word of Caution

In the effort to be modest and discrete in dress and makeup, it is easy to become so rigid that you do not enjoy the freedom

God has given you. First Peter 3:3 says, "Your adornment must not be *merely* external. . . ." It is all right to have some external adornment, because stripping oneself of all makeup and wearing only plain, drab clothing does not make a woman more pleasing to God. If she thinks it does, she is "delighting in self-abasement" (Col. 2:18). Her pseudo-spirituality becomes "matters which have, to be sure, the appearance of wisdom in self-made religion and self-abasement . . . but are of no value against fleshly indulgence" (Col. 2:23). So, do not be legalistic about dress and makeup. Enjoy the freedom the Lord has given you in this area, but use that freedom within the bounds of the biblical principles that we have explained.

Conclusion

We must turn our passion from loving ourselves and calling attention to ourselves to a passion for God and serving Him regardless of what we look like. We must thank God for what we look like and gratefully grow old graciously. We should leave a legacy for our daughters and the younger women in our church that the Lord Jesus was our passion, not what we looked like. Instead of living as vain, proud women, our lives should be "a living and holy sacrifice" for our Lord (Rom. 12:1).

Vanity is the love of beauty. It is funny to think about Narcissus turning into a daffodil. But it is not so funny when we think about how very ugly we are to God when we love ourselves like the daughters of Zion did instead of loving Him with all our heart, soul, mind, and strength.

Where is your heart? What is really important to you? How much time do you spend thinking about what you look like and what others think of you? How much time do you spend comparing yourself to others or bemoaning your weight? The pagans (unbelievers) love and cherish themselves. We are to love and cherish the Lord Jesus and be glad for Him to use us however He chooses—no matter what we look like.

~~~~~~~~ *Study Questions* ~~~~~~~~

1. The Jewish women in Isaiah's day had turned from serving the one, true God. God warned them through the prophet Isaiah that judgment would come. What was the judgment? See Isaiah 3:16–24.

2. Make a list from the chart on page 92 of signs of vanity in yourself. Can you think of other signs?

3. What is the Old Testament emphasis concerning vanity? Instead of being vain, what should describe a godly woman?

4. What is the New Testament emphasis concerning vanity? What should a godly woman's adornment be?

5. According to 1 Timothy 2:9–10, what describes "proper clothing"?

6. Give several examples of good works that you could do for others.

7. What does having a "gentle and quiet spirit" mean?

8. Match the following characteristics of a vain woman with the appropriate Scripture:

She is not content.	1 Timothy 6:6
She thinks too highly of herself.	James 1:14–15
She is not grateful.	1 John 2:15–17
She is tempted to sin by her own lust for beauty.	1 Thessalonians 5:16–18
She is motivated by a love for the world.	Romans 12:3

9. Who is our most precious example of godly beauty?

10. What are some of the scriptural warnings regarding vanity?

11. Refer back to question 2. What is your prayer?

7

Are You Sure PMS Is Real?

PMS

It is generally thought that PMS is a license to go berserk. Everyone knows that some women have great difficulties with relationships and their emotions when they experience PMS. A very "laid back" woman who has no problems with PMS is rare. When I was a counselor to women at the Atlanta Biblical Counseling Center, ladies often would include PMS in their list of presenting problems. Some would fly into angry rages, others into panic attacks. Many would become sad and depressed. Just as the duration and intensity of cramping with the onset of a menstrual period varies in intensity, so do the miserable emotions before the period actually begins.

When I was a young wife and mother (before I was a Christian), I remember feeling discouraged, sorry for myself, and paranoid during the week leading up to my period. This was really strange because normally I was the opposite. However, one aspect of my personality was true to form during the PMS time, and that was my tendency to become angry and impatient. The frustration and irritation I would feel would sometimes spin completely out of control. I was, in a word, berserk!

After the Lord saved me, my PMS symptoms continued, but as my anger and impatience subsided due to God's grace, so did some of my bad feelings and actions before my period. Then I had the Lord and His Word to cling to, and to the degree that I did that and honored Him in spite of my feelings, I got through that PMS time fairly well.

What does God want to teach us during these times? How can we endure those times in a God-honoring way that is pleasing to Him? Let's begin with a short medical definition and treatment plan for PMS, and then lay out a biblical plan of action. PMS *is* real but so is our hope in the Lord.

Definition, Symptoms, and Treatment

According to one medical journal, here is how doctors define PMS:

> Premenstrual Syndrome (PMS) refers to a group of menstrually related disorders and symptoms that include premenstrual dysphoric [unpleasant physical and emotional symptoms] disorder as well as affective disturbances [transient feelings and behavior], alterations in appetite, cognitive disturbances [ability to think], fluid retention and various types of pain.[1]

In other words, in the last week to ten days before your period begins, you have the symptoms. Once your period actually begins, the PMS symptoms quickly subside.

Symptoms include fluid retention, insomnia, nightmares, hot flashes, gastrointestinal disturbances, heart palpitations, dizziness, and hypoglycemic symptoms (headache, fatigue, cravings for sweet or salt). In addition, there are mood changes such as increased anger, anxiety, frustration, or depression.

Upon looking through several medical journals, I found that there are different ways to treat PMS. *All agreed that general measures very often will decrease or completely alleviate symptoms of PMS.* The general measures were exercise, diet, and supportive therapy (a friend to talk to). Usually two or three paragraphs were devoted to general measures. How they treated medications, however, was a different matter.

In the journals, there were page after page of medications which, they admitted, did not always work and sometimes made things worse. There were diuretics for swelling, non-steroidals for physical discomfort, birth control pills to try to stabilize the hormones, and psychotropic drugs for emotional discomfort. The journals said that birth control pills helped twenty-five percent of women, fifty percent stayed the same, and twenty-five percent got worse. The psychotropic drugs such as tranquilizers (such as Xanax) and anti-depressants (such as Prozac) possibly could help with some of the symptoms but could also make the symptoms worse. For example, a major side effect of Prozac is anxiety. For the woman who is already struggling with anxiety, this could end up being her worst nightmare.[2]

Sometimes people ask me if I think PMS is real. The answer is "Yes!" but as real as it is, it cannot prevent us from honoring God and loving others during that time. So, let's turn to a biblical plan of action to deal with the PMS mess.

A Biblical Plan of Action

1. Make an honest assessment of your character weaknesses. If you are naturally a worrier or easily irritated, you will be worse in the days before your period begins. If you are a person who is somewhat melancholy, you will likely be much more sad and discouraged. Whatever your weaknesses, they will be exaggerated. So, these areas will be something you need to work on. And with God's help, you can change.

2. Write a self-talk log. Whenever you feel sad or irritated or nervous or anxious, write down what you are thinking. Then analyze each thought based on Scripture and write out a God-honoring thought instead. Consider the examples in figure 7.1.

3. Realize that the mood swings are real and difficult, but are not an excuse to sin. Before the Lord Jesus died, He told His disciples not to be afraid, that He would be back, and that God the Father would send another Helper who would be with them forever—the Holy Spirit (John 14:16–17). We know from later

Fig. 7.1 Self-Talk Log

Biblical Criteria for Thoughts (Phil. 4:8)	Example of Wrong Thought	Example of God-honoring Thought
True (faces reality, but with a hope in God)	*Nobody cares about me.*	*I feel like nobody cares about me, but the truth is a lot of people do, and the Lord does most of all.* (1 Peter 5:7)
Honorable (honoring to God)	*Why doesn't God help me? After all I've done for Him, look what I get.*	*Lord, forgive me for maligning You. Instead, use me for your glory however you choose. If the PMS symptoms have to continue, they'll just have to continue. I want to glorify You.*
Lovely (assumes the best)	*My husband doesn't love me. He says he does, but he doesn't really mean it.*	*I feel as if he doesn't love me, but I know my feelings will change when my period starts. Therefore, I am going to go against my feelings and assume the best about him.* (1 Cor. 13:7)
Excellent and Worthy of Praise (points to God)	*I can't take it any more. There is no hope.*	*With God's help I can stay in my circumstances and not sin against Him. He will not let me be pressured beyond what I can stand.* (1 Cor. 10:13)

Scriptures that the Holy Spirit indwells all believers and helps them not to sin. When God saves us, He renders powerless the grip that sin previously had on us. Even though we will still sin until we go to be with the Lord, we do not have to give in to temptation. Paul wrote:

> Even so consider yourselves to be dead to sin, but alive to God in Christ Jesus. Therefore do not let sin reign in your mortal body so that you obey its lusts, and do not go on presenting the members of your body to sin as instruments of unrighteousness; but present yourselves to God as those alive from the dead, and your members as instruments of righteousness to God. (Rom. 6:11–13)

4. Plan and maintain your diet and exercise. There are many practical things you can do without even going to the doctor. Go completely off caffeine for at least ten days before your period. That also means going off chocolate (sorry!), because chocolate contains caffeine. Eat a good balanced diet with smaller but more frequent meals. This will help your blood sugar level remain stable. Try to do some form of mild, aerobic exercise for fifteen to twenty minutes daily during those ten days. That means going for a brisk walk or exercising with a television, DVD, or videotape exercise program. You do not have to go to an aerobics class or join a gym unless you want to. If just changing your diet and exercise during those days will take the edge off, then it seems foolish to take mind-altering medications that are expensive, potentially harmful with very serious side effects, and often very difficult to come off of.

5. Plan your calendar wisely. Mark your calendar ahead for when you anticipate your period. If you are on a twenty-eight-day cycle, begin counting the days on the first day of your last period. When you get to day twenty-eight, then count backward seven to ten days and mark those days as probable PMS days. If possible, do not plan unnecessary stressful events during that time. Perhaps a large dinner party can be scheduled for a different week or the out-of-town guests can be flexible. Certainly never wait until the last moment (which could be your PMS time) to do your Christmas shopping.

6. *Plan for extra rest.* Some women benefit from a brief nap during their PMS days. If you have children, scheduling rest or naps in the afternoon will help. However, do not let this be an excuse to lazily lie around in bed or watch soap operas and become even more depressed. Set your alarm, and then get up and get to work after your rest.

7. *Ask your husband or a godly older woman for help.* Since Christians are to help each other bear one another's burdens of sin, find someone who is close to you and ask for help. Ask him or her to hold you accountable to think and act in a godly manner and to point out times when you are out of line. Whoever does this for you should be kind and tenderhearted, but firm and straightforward. This can be one of the ways that your husband lives with you "in an understanding way" (1 Peter 3:7).

PMS symptoms are generally miserable and not something that a woman can just "snap out of." So, whoever is holding you accountable should be patient and empathetic and should not desire to return "evil for evil . . . but [give] a blessing instead" (1 Peter 3:9). His or her goal should be to help restore you to a right relationship with God and with others.

8. *Together with the person holding you accountable, make a plan of how they will actually help.* Figure 7.2 is one example.

Fig. 7.2 Plan of Accountability

Remind me of Scripture	• Recite from memory or read Hebrews 4:15–16. • Remind me that this is one of my times of need. • Remind me to ask God to help.
Pray for and with me	• That I will honor God in my thinking in spite of how I feel. (Phil. 4:8) • That I will be kind and tenderhearted instead of angry and bitter. (Eph. 4:30–32) • That my love will abound still more and more in real knowledge and discernment. (Phil. 1:9) • That the fruit of the Spirit will be shown in my life for the praise and glory of God's grace. (Gal. 5:22–23; Eph. 1:6) • That I won't look out just for my own interests but for the interests of others. (Phil. 2:4) • That I will do all things without grumbling and complaining. (Phil. 2:14)
Give me hope	• Read Scriptures that will remind me of the goodness of God and His purposes in my life. (Rom. 8:28–29; 1 Cor. 10:13; Lam. 3:21–25)
Remind me that I do not have to sin; I can glorify God.	• If I honor God and go against how I feel, there will be blessings now (emotional stability and getting along well with others) and in eternity (rewards at the judgment seat of Christ). (1 Cor. 3:10–15) • There is nothing that can prevent me from giving God glory. (1 Cor. 10:31) • As a believer, the power grip of sin in my life has been broken. (Rom. 6:11–14)
Read Psalms aloud to me or have me read them aloud	• Instruct me that the Psalms are God's tranquilizers for my soul. In them I will find others who have struggled with emotional pain and difficult circumstances. One example is Psalm 73:25–28: "Whom have I in heaven but You? And besides You, I desire nothing on earth. My flesh and my heart may fail, But God is the strength of my heart and my portion forever. . . . But as for me, the nearness of God is my good; I have made the Lord God my refuge, That I may tell of all Your works."
Remind me to keep short accounts of sin and thereby draw near to God	• I can have the joy of knowing that I am honoring the Lord in spite of how I feel. • God is faithful to forgive me. (1 John 1:9) • As I draw near to God, He promises to draw near to me. (James 4:8–10) • When I sin, my bad feelings will be intensified, thus creating unnecessary emotional pain and making it more difficult not to sin. • Ask God to help me bridle my tongue and not sin against Him during this time. (James 1:19–20)

Whether you have someone to hold you accountable or not, you are still responsible before God to do the right thing. If there is no one to help you, you can make a chart for yourself and go over it alone when you are struggling.

9. *If needed, go to the doctor.* Your doctor can make sure that you have no additional physical problems such as hypoglycemia or a thyroid problem, or a side effect of a medicine you are already taking that is creating more depression or anxiety (for example, birth control pills, steroids, or blood pressure medicine).

10. *Maintain an organized home and schedule.* A clean, organized home will help you make it through those days when you feel muddled, confused, and overwhelmed. Always have two or three simple, quick meals on hand to prepare for those difficult days. Already having most of the clothes cleaned, folded, put away, or ironed and hanging in the closet will be a special blessing on difficult days. Already know where your car keys are because you left them where they belong. Already have gas in the car because you stopped and filled up before the gas gage was empty. Working hard at being organized all along makes life easier when there are PMS bumps in the road.

11. *Turn your focus from yourself to God and others.*

- Pray for others.
- Thank God for . . .
- Fulfill your responsibilities whether you feel like it or not.
- Sing praise songs and hymns, or play them from a tape or CD.
- Tell God you love Him, trust Him, and that He is good.
- Work on new or review older Scripture memory.

Conclusion

PMS is real. And because of our hormones *and* our sin, we can act like Dr. Jekyll or Mr. Hyde. Our sinful tendencies will be exaggerated and we will be tested in ways that normally would not bother us at all, or certainly to a much lesser degree. We have seen many practical things you can do that will help you, but the underlying key during the days of PMS is having a right relationship to God, and so delighting in Him and what He is doing in your life that the painful emotions will not overwhelm you.

The Lord Jesus knows our weaknesses; He is our ever present help. He invites you to come boldly to His throne of grace and there "receive mercy and find grace to help" when you need Him (Heb. 4:16). Listen to David's psalm:

O LORD, You have searched me and known me.
You know when I sit down and when I rise up;
You understand my thought from afar.
You scrutinize my path and my lying down,
And are intimately acquainted with all my ways.
Even before there is a word on my tongue,
Behold, O LORD, You know it all.
You have enclosed me behind and before,
And laid Your hand upon me.
Such knowledge is too wonderful for me;
It is too high, I cannot attain to it. . . .

For You formed my inward parts;
You wove me in my mother's womb.
I will give thanks to You, for I am fearfully and wonder-
  fully made;
Wonderful are Your works,

And my soul knows it very well.
My frame was not hidden from You,
When I was made in secret,
And skillfully wrought in the depths of the earth;
Your eyes have seen my unformed substance;
And in Your book were all written
The days that were ordained for me,
When as yet there was not one of them.

How precious also are Your thoughts to me, O God!
How vast is the sum of them!
If I should count them, they would outnumber the sand.
When I awake, I am still with You. . . .

Search me, O God, and know my heart;
Try me and know my anxious thoughts;
And see if there be any hurtful way in me,
And lead me in the everlasting way. (Ps. 139:1–6, 13–18,
   23–24)

Study Questions

1. What does PMS stand for?
2. True or False:
   a. The PMS symptoms begin the day your menstrual
      period begins.
   b. The only way to treat PMS is with medication.
   c. Women who naturally are worriers will likely be very
      worried or anxious during the PMS time of their cycle.
   d. It is common for women to feel sorry for themselves
      during the PMS time of their cycle.
   e. It's OK to act on how you feel.

3. Make a list of the practical actions that a woman may do to help with her PMS symptoms.

4. How would you explain, "plan your calendar wisely."

5. Make a personal plan of action for the person holding you accountable. You may use all or parts of the chart beginning on page 109 or you may create your own chart. Be sure to include several Scriptures in your plan.

6. What does maintaining an organized home have to do with honoring God during your premenstrual cycle?

7. What are some specific ways you can turn your focus from yourself to a focus on God and others?

8

I Just Love Rules, Don't You?

LEGALISM

Our daughter, Anna, attended a well-known Bible college back in the 1980s. At that school they had a rather thick rule book. To her dismay, she broke four of the rules before she even had time to read the book! Not being a rebel in her heart, Anna had no problem keeping the rules once she knew what they were, but what she did have a problem with were those students who loved the rules so much that they became like self-appointed, private investigators looking to trap and turn in students who broke or appeared to break the slightest rule. These students became like the Pharisees of Jesus' day who were religious in a bad sense. The students and the Pharisees became amazingly creative in their ability to make up religious rules that they thought saved them or made them more pleasing to God. Usually accompanying those self-imposed standards was a disdain for those who did not follow their rules, a sense of superiority over others, an unbiblical view of grace, and fear of consequences if they did not do everything just right.

The modern-day legalist is a lot like those students and the Pharisees. The legalist is drawn toward unbiblical thinking—so much so that there are strong Scriptural warnings against such man-made religion:

> "Watch out! Beware of the leaven of the Pharisees. . . ." (Mark 8:15)

> See to it that no one takes you captive through philosophy and empty deception, according to the tradition of men, according to the elementary principles of the world, rather than according to Christ. (Col. 2:8)

> Do not be carried away by varied and strange teachings; for it is good for the heart to be strengthened by grace, not by foods, through which those who were so occupied were not benefited. (Heb. 13:9)

The life of legalists is not the joyous Christian walk that God intends. It is a life of burden for themselves and the others they influence. Martin Luther vividly described the mindset of the legalist: "Christ's a fine Master. He makes the beginning, but Moses [the Old Testament Law] must complete the structure. The devil's nature shows itself therein: [if] he cannot ruin people by wronging and persecuting them, he will do it by improving them."[1] In this chapter we want to cover what the Bible teaches about legalism, typical legalistic thoughts and actions, and how to overcome the sinful bent to add to God's standard of righteousness.

What the Bible Teaches about Legalism

The Pharisees were a Jewish religious sect that evolved into a very rigid, self-righteous, letter of (their) law group. They were thought to be the epitome of righteousness. They hated the Lord Jesus because He saw through their façade and knew their hearts. The Pharisees made up hundreds of new laws that they were comfortable keeping. In order to justify observing certain laws and not others, they divided God's Law into greater laws (that they kept) and lesser laws (that were in their opinion optional). The laws that they arbitrarily decided were the "greater" laws were, of course, the ones they would not have broken anyway.

The Old Testament Pharisee and the modern-day legalist are a lot alike. They are both sinfully proud. They think they can earn God's favor or that they deserve it in some way, and they look down on those who are not as "spiritual" as they think they are. Legalism is a vivid example of *not* trusting in the Lord, but instead leaning on your own understanding (see Prov. 3:5).

Biblical Principles Concerning Legalism[2]

To understand legalism, let's look at twelve biblical principles:

1. *Legalism aims to attain spirituality by means of what one does or does not do.* A legalist establishes an external standard of spirituality and then judges everyone by that standard. Since the individual has established the standard, normally that person always achieves it:[3]

> For not knowing about God's righteousness and seeking to establish their own, they did not subject themselves to the righteousness of God. (Rom. 10:3)

2. The Law is a divine rule or commandment. Often when people say *the* Law, they are referring to the Ten Commandments or to the entire Mosaic Law located in the first five books of the Bible:

> Then the Lord said to Moses, "Thus you shall say to the sons of Israel, 'You yourselves have seen that I have spoken to you from heaven. You shall not make other gods besides Me. . . .' " (Ex. 20:22–23)

3. The Law has three aspects:

a. The sacrificial system: The Jews would bring animals for sacrifice and the priests would carry out the sacrifice. There were varying reasons for the different sacrifices, but the main reason was as a guilt offering to atone for Israel's sin. This is no longer necessary because the sacrifice was fulfilled in the Lord Jesus Christ:

> For it was fitting for us to have such a high priest, holy, innocent, undefiled, separated from sinners and exalted above the heavens; who does not need daily, like those high priests, to offer up sacrifices, first for His own sins and then for the sins of the people, because this He did once for all when He offered up Himself. (Heb. 7:26–27)

b. The civil law: The civil law was given to the nation of Israel in the Old Testament. There were many civil laws, including dietary laws, laws dictating which years to let the land rest from planting crops, and laws telling how many days after a male baby's birth he was to be circumcised. We are no longer under the civil laws:

But some of the sect of the Pharisees who had believed stood up, saying, "It is necessary to circumcise them and to direct them to observe the Law of Moses."

The apostles and the elders came together to look into this matter. After there had been much debate Peter stood up and said to them . . . "But we believe that we are saved through the grace of the Lord Jesus, in the same way as they also are." (Acts 15:5–7, 11)

c. *The moral law:* We, like those in the Old Testament times, are under the moral law of God. For example, we are told not to commit adultery in the Old Testament, and the New Testament standard is the same. In fact, the Lord Jesus further explained that we are not even to lust in our hearts. The moral law of God convicts us, restrains sin in society, and is the rule of life for the believer:

Then God spoke all these words saying, "I am the LORD your God, who brought you out of the land of Egypt, out of the house of slavery. . . . You shall not commit adultery." (Ex. 20:1, 14)

"You have heard that it was said, 'YOU SHALL NOT COMMIT ADULTERY'; but I [the Lord] say to you that everyone who looks at a woman with lust for her has already committed adultery with her in his heart." (Matt. 5:27–28)

4. *God has provided all the resources for man's salvation from sin.* The Lord Jesus Christ, God in the flesh, is the only provision for sinful man's salvation that is acceptable to God. Christ obeyed God's Law perfectly by living the sinless life that we should live but cannot. God's provision for salvation is unde-

served by man. Because of sin, man deserves condemnation. Because of God's gracious provision, man can be saved but only through faith in Christ alone:

> For what the Law could not do, weak as it was through the flesh, God did: sending His own son in the likeness of sinful flesh and as an offering for sin, He condemned sin in the flesh, so that the requirement of the Law might be fulfilled in us, who do not walk according to the flesh but according to the Spirit. (Rom. 8:3–4)

5. *Liberty is the life of the Christian under the control of the Holy Spirit.* In Christ the believer is free to live a life pleasing to God no longer under the penalty and power of sin.

> For if we have become united with Him in the likeness of His death, certainly we shall also be in the likeness of His resurrection, knowing this, that our old self was crucified with Him, in order that our body of sin might be done away with, so that we would no longer be slaves to sin; for he who has died is freed from sin. (Rom. 6:5–7)

6. *Legalism is an unbiblical response to the law of God.* The unbiblical response to God's law is man's attempt to add his own good works to God's grace. In so doing man seeks to conform to a code for the purpose of glorifying self:

> Now that no one is justified by the Law before God is evident; for, "THE RIGHTEOUS MAN SHALL LIVE BY FAITH." (Gal. 3:11)

7. *The problem with legalism is in man's heart (what he thinks).* The natural heart is a legalistic heart; man thinks he can help God or make God a debtor to him, or that he deserves what God has done for him. It is pride that keeps us from seeing our sin and how utterly dependent we are on God to do the work of our salvation:

> But a natural man does not accept the things of the Spirit of God, for they are foolishness to him; and he cannot understand them, because they are spiritually appraised. (1 Cor. 2:14)

8. *Because of man's nature and his propensity to sin, he wants to make the Christian life workable in the flesh.* The legalist looks for techniques and formulas (step one, step two . . .). Commands are too general. He thinks he needs more organization concerning the answer to the complexities of life. Some modern-day examples are "steps to find God's will" or "witness to X number of people each day" or "clothing must be a certain style" or "abstain from certain foods":

> Do not tear down the work of God for the sake of food. . . . (Rom. 14:20)

9. *Legalism is any attempt to change people through conformity to rules.* Churches that are unbiblically authoritarian often do this.

> Therefore, I exhort the elders among you, as your fellow elder and witness of the sufferings of Christ, and a partaker also of the glory that is to be revealed, shepherd the flock of God among you, exercising oversight

not under compulsion, but voluntarily, according to
the will of God; and not for sordid gain, but with
eagerness; nor yet as lording it over those allotted to
your charge, but proving to be examples to the flock.
(1 Peter 5:1–3)

10. *Legalism is manifested in a variety of ways:* men think
their acts should gain God's favor because God is somehow
obligated to them; men outwardly go through the motions of
vain, repetitious religion; men commit acts based only on
human wisdom and strength without regard to the Word of
God or the Holy Spirit:

> See to it that no one takes you captive through philoso-
> phy and empty deception, according to the tradition of
> men, according to the elementary principles of the
> world, rather than according to Christ. (Col. 2:8)

11. *Legalism is an unbiblical response to the Old Testament
narrative stories.* This code may be biblical or man-made.
Legalists often go to Old Testament narrative stories, miss the
point, and make their rules in relation to the story. Examples are
dietary rules, courtship rules, and promises made because of
parental "blessings."

> So Isaac called Jacob and blessed him and charged him,
> and said to him, "You shall not take a wife from the
> daughters of Canaan. Arise, go to Paddan-aram, to the
> house of Bethuel your mother's father; and from there
> take to yourself a wife from the daughters of Laban your
> mother's brother. May God Almighty bless you and
> make you fruitful and multiply you, that you may

become a company of peoples. May He also give you the blessing of Abraham, to you and to your descendants with you, that you may possess the land of your sojournings, which God gave to Abraham." (Gen. 28:1–4)

All Scripture is "profitable for teaching" us, but not all Scripture is written *about* us or *to* us (see 2 Tim. 3:16). Thus, parents who make up certain rules or special promised "blessings" for their child based on Old Testament narrative stories such as Isaac's blessings to Jacob are missing the point of the passage. The point is what God is doing to fulfill His covenant promises to the children of Israel. Sometimes parents unintentionally misuse the passage and place an unbiblical burden of man-made rules or false expectations on their child.

Another example would be courtship rules. Having personal standards and family traditions such as the young man asking the father's permission before asking the young lady out is fine. Not dating in a frivolous way is fine. What is not fine is thinking that these personal standards are a God-mandated rule that guarantees success in the marriage. Instead of hard-and-fast rules, the biblical standard is wisdom, discernment, marrying only a Christian, chastity before marriage, and knowing that both the child and his or her spouse will sin—but there are biblical ways to deal with their sin. So, have standards and base them on biblical principles. but do not elevate them to a "thus said the Lord" level.

12. Legalism seeks to exalt self and gain merit rather than to glorify God because of what He has done. The power source is *self* not the Holy Spirit. Israel fell into this kind of legalism:

"When you pray, you are not to be like the hypocrites; for they love to stand and pray in the synagogues and on the street corners so that they may be seen by men. Truly I say to you, they have their reward in full. But you, when you pray, go into your inner room, close your door and pray to your Father who is in secret, and your Father who sees what is done in secret will reward you.

"And when you are praying, do not use meaningless repetition as the Gentiles do, for they suppose that they will be heard for their many words." (Matt. 6:5–7)

What Legalism Does

There are many problems with legalism. Consider the following list:

- Legalism takes our attention off Jesus Christ by focusing on our own efforts rather than what He has done for us.
- Legalism takes away the believer's freedom by substituting conformity for control by the Spirit.
- Legalism attempts to put God in the position of being a debtor. It thinks God owes us something when we do good.
- Legalism results in regression in the Christian life.
- Legalism is performance-oriented. It focuses more on what one does than on who one is.
- Legalism brings about harshness and conflict in one's relationships. The reason for this is because legalism creates an elitist attitude in which conformity is demanded and failure is not tolerated.
- Legalism will rob a Christian of joy, for he will never know the "rest" that faith brings. A legalist is so intent on *doing* that he does not know how to *enjoy* God's acceptance.
- Legalists are very zealous. This is why legalism brings results, but the results are counterfeits.

- Legalism is selective in the matters it chooses and promotes. It will take parts of God's Law but ignore the rest. It is never consistent. An interesting aspect is not what legalism forbids but what it overlooks.

- Legalism will affect everything if unchecked. Given time it will control everything—individual churches, schools, and denominations.

- Legalism attacks grace. Legalists will accuse those who preach grace of being antinomian (lawless). But this cannot be true because what grace really does is strip away any pretense of spiritual achievement. Grace promotes obedience to God because of His blessings to us. Grace is a license to serve, not a license to sin.

- Legalism is inflexible and condemnatory. It refuses to see many, if any, gray areas in the Christian life. Legalists have rules for almost every area of life and have a negative judgmental attitude toward those who do not comply with their standards. This can result in a very tense environment.

- Legalism promotes pride and self-righteousness. Of course the legalist denies this, but it is true nevertheless.

- Legalism opts for a lower standard than God's. The kind of legalism that emphasizes many man-made rules becomes satisfied with what is really an inferior standard. Consider the following vivid contrast between man-made rules and God's high and holy law. Man-made rules: don't wear jewelry or makeup or denim clothing, burn your secular music because it has demons in it, don't practice any birth control, insist that men's hair must be above their ears. God's Law: love God and love others.

Why Is Scripture So against Legalism?

Legalists can appear to others (and certainly to themselves) to be so godly. Their emphasis is on minor, little things, but they miss the heart and real intention of God's law such as hospitality, love, caring for widows and orphans, generosity, kindness, justice, and mercy. No wonder the Lord Jesus admonished them strongly, "Woe to you, scribes and Pharisees, hypocrites! For you tithe mint and dill and cumin, and have neglected the *weightier provisions of the law*: justice and mercy and faithfulness . . ." (Matt. 23:23).

Legalism also creates a proud person: "I'm keeping the rules so I must be spiritual." The Lord Jesus shocked the people who thought there were none more righteous than the Pharisees, "For I say to you that unless your righteousness surpasses that of the scribes and Pharisees, you will not enter the kingdom of heaven" (Matt. 5:20). In other words, they had to have perfect righteousness, which, of course, only God could do for them.

Legalism creates self-righteousness. It looks down on those not as spiritual as we are. We see this example in the Scriptures when the Lord Jesus ate with the tax collectors and sinners, and the Pharisees questioned His disciples. When Jesus heard about what was being said, He said, "It is not those who are healthy who need a physician, but those who are sick. But go and learn what this means: 'I DESIRE COMPASSION, AND NOT SACRIFICE,' for I did not come to call the righteous, but sinners" (Matt. 9:12–13). The Pharisees should have been glad that the "sinners" could spend time with our Lord.

Legalism emphasizes outward show. Remember the Pharisee who stood on the street corner praying out loud thanking God that he was not like the sinner standing nearby? The Lord Jesus said that legalists were like tombstones that were whitewashed and gleaming on the outside but were full of dead men's bones on the inside. He told them, "So you, too, outwardly appear righteous to men, but inwardly you are full of hypocrisy and lawlessness" (Matt. 23:28). Just about anyone can manage to put on an outward show at least for a little while, but the true believer wants the attention called to God not himself.

Legalism can become very rigid and crowd out love. Legalistic homes will often lack love because they have a lot of rules and rigidity. One legalistic rule they might have, for example, is that a girl should not marry a man who has been a Christian for less time than she has. Parents can exasperate children because the parents see their rules as "thus saith the Lord," instead of recognizing areas where their children have freedom in the Lord to differ with others.

Legalism can create a dependence on human leaders. It is common for Christians to follow a man (or a movement) because he provides a new set of regulations for given situations. People turn to this kind of leader rather than turn to the Word of God through personal study. People can be held in emotional bondage to such leaders because they will sometimes say, "It's OK for you to do that but if you *really* want God's best then. . . ." Well, who wouldn't want God's best? Even though it may *appear* to be the legalist who desires God's best, it is not. What legalists really desire is making themselves look good.

Remember that you should not automatically label someone a legalist just because he or she has different rules or follows a more rigid lifestyle. Legalists have a wrong *attitude* toward their rules. They add rules to the gospel or to how we grow as Christians. They tend to be rigid, angry, harsh, and often self-righteous instead of loving, kind, and gentle. Churches and Christian schools must have rules. Rules help us live together and they protect us. So, do not automatically write off a church or school because they have rules. The question to consider is: What is their attitude toward their rules?

Scripture soundly condemns those who have external, lip-service religion but whose hearts are far away from God. The strong believer (the one who understands his liberty in Christ and knows how to exercise it responsibly) has an obligation to the weaker brother (the legalistic kind). He must love him and seek to help him understand his freedom in Christ and the relationship between law and grace. We are to exemplify true biblical Christianity, not just criticize legalists. Our lives should model God's grace at work in our hearts.

A Model of God's Grace

Read the following list and see if in your heart you are a model of God's grace or a Pharisee.[4]

1. Do you take seriously the total corruption of your human nature? This does not mean that every person will be as bad as they could possibly be, but it does mean that all of your nature has been affected by sin (your will, intellect, affections, and conscience). (Gen. 6:5)
2. Do you believe that the Bible alone is the inspired Word of God and authoritative over your life? (2 Tim. 3:16–17)
3. Do you have a right respect for the atoning work of the Lord Jesus Christ on the cross, understanding that you cannot add anything to His work? Not even baptism, communion, ceremonial acts of worship, or perfect church attendance? (Eph. 2:1–10)
4. Do you give God credit for any fruit in your life, knowing that it is the Holy Spirit who produces such fruit? (Gal. 5:13–23)

5. Do you view life through the lens of loving God and loving others? (Matt. 22:35–40)

6. Would you patiently teach younger Christians, or would you try to impose standards on them in areas where God has given us freedom?

7. Are you discerning between "thus saith the Lord" and your own personal standards? For example: women are to be modest in dress versus women cannot wear eye shadow.

8. Are you more likely to think, *I'm glad I'm not like so-and-so . . .* or to think, *It is only by God's grace that I am not worse than so-and-so. I will pray for her.*

9. Do you have disdain for others, thinking, *I would* never *do what she did,* or do you have compassion and think, *Because of my sin nature, I am capable of doing something worse. How can I help her?*

10. Would you be horrified if you saw your friend's daughter at church and she had on a toe ring? Or would you think, *Well, that's not me, but it is not a sin to wear a toe ring. This is an area where we both have freedom, me not to wear one and she to wear one.*

11. Would your first reaction to a church's music that you did not approve of be, "That music is awful. They must not be Christians!" or would it be, "Just because I do not like their music certainly does not mean they are not Christians."

12. Do you believe that if you wear makeup you are out of God's will, or do you think that makeup is a matter of "freedom in the Lord," and you can enjoy that freedom?

13. Have you been discouraged, thinking, *If I don't read my Bible every day, I must not be a Christian,* or if you miss a day reading the Bible, do you think, *Certainly God wants me to read my Bible every day, but He accom-*

plished the work of my salvation on the cross. I cannot add to or keep my salvation by reading the Bible.

14. Have you found yourself suspicious of another woman's spirituality or salvation if her hair is short? Or do you realize that hair styles are cultural and this is an area where she has freedom in the Lord?

15. Have you ever thought or said, "My child would never do what her child just did"? or would you be quick to think, *As far as I know, my child has never done what her child did, but that does not mean that he won't do it or something worse in the future.*

16. Are you drawn toward systems that are full of rules, such as "courtship," thinking that if you follow the rules just right, God will have to bless your children's marriages? Or do you realize that courtship is not a "thus saith the Lord" issue, but is based on man-made rules drawn from Old Testament stories. What is biblical is wisdom, discernment, marrying only a Christian, chastity before marriage, and knowing that both your child and his or her spouse will sin—but there are biblical ways to deal with it.

17. Have you ever thought, *If I overeat (or any other sin), God will be mad at me, and I must not be saved,* or would you think, *My salvation does not now nor did it ever depend on what I eat. I must believe God when His Word says, "If we confess our sins, He is faithful and righteous to forgive us our sins and to cleanse us from all unrighteousness"* (1 John 1:9).

Conclusion

The legalist thinks that her outward religious activities will cause God to be obligated to save her or, if not that, then at least she will be more pleasing to God if she keeps her rules and regulations. We have seen that instead of having disdain for those who do not follow our rules, we must put up with non-sinful differences; instead of having a sense of superiority over others, we must have humble compassion, understanding that we could be worse than they; instead of holding to an unbiblical view of God's grace, our lives should be a model of God's grace; and instead of fearing the consequences if we do not do everything just right, we should enjoy the freedoms the Lord has given us and be grateful for the forgiveness we have in Christ.

Do not too quickly label people as legalists just because they have stricter or different personal standards than you. Legalism is not what you or they *do* but what you or they *think* about what you do. The legalistic heart is in bondage to a sinful system of spirituality. If this is a problem in your heart, you must repent and come out of the darkness of self-righteousness and into the light of God's glorious grace.

⸙⸙⸙⸙⸙⸙⸙ *Study Questions* ⸙⸙⸙⸙⸙⸙⸙

1. Why did the Pharisees divide God's laws into *greater* laws and *lesser* laws?

2. Match the following:

Legalists establish their own righteousness.	Matthew 5:27–28
Animal sacrifices are no longer necessary to atone for sin because of the Lord Jesus Christ's death on the cross.	Romans 8:3–4
The Pharisees wanted to keep Christians under bondage to circumcision.	Romans 6:5–7
The moral law of God convicts us, restrains sin in society, and is a rule of life for the believer.	Acts 15:5–11
The Lord Jesus Christ, not the Law, is the only provision for sinful man's salvation that is acceptable to God.	Romans 10:3
The believer is no longer under bondage to sin.	Hebrews 7:26–27

3. According to Galatians 3:11, how is the righteous man *not* justified? How is he to live?

4. According to principle 8 on page 121, what is wrong with techniques and formulas?

5. What are some of the ways legalism is manifested? (See principle 10 on page 122.)

6. What is wrong with making rules from narrative stories from the Old Testament? (See principle 11 on page 122.)

7. Make a brief summary of the problems with legalism from the "What Legalism Does" list.

8. Reread the questions from the list "A Model of God's Grace." Write down the areas where you know you are guilty. Look up the Scripture at the end of each question. Think about and write down what you *should* be thinking or doing instead.

9. What is your prayer?

PART THREE

⌘

Biblical Solutions for Problems with the World

⌘

"Do not love the world nor the things in the world. If anyone loves the world, the love of the Father is not in him." 1 John 2:15

9

But What If I *Like* to Have My Ears Tickled?

THE FEMINIST INFLUENCE

All my life I have been influenced by what others think and do. We all have. Thinking back over my childhood, I can remember believing that everything my parents thought was absolute truth. So, it was quite unsettling for me the first time I realized they were wrong about something. As I got older, though, I was less and less influenced by my parents and more and more influenced by television, education, and friends. I graduated from high school and nursing school in the sixties. Those were the years of the Vietnam War, the sexual revolution, and the beginnings of the modern feminist movement.

The feminist movement in America began more than a hundred years ago primarily embracing voting rights and equal rights of property ownership for husband and wife, but by the 1960s the focus had turned to other issues. The overriding issue became the woman's right to mature to "full human identity."[1] A young woman named Betty Friedan articulated very clearly her personal search for meaning in a book she wrote entitled *The Feminine Mystique*.

135

The Feminine Mystique took America by storm. Thousands of men and women read it. Almost everyone was talking about it. It was the subject of newspaper editorials, television news stories, beauty parlor chit-chat, and women's magazine articles. Very quickly men became chauvinist pigs and women became either freedom fighters or doormats. Friedan's beliefs impacted everyone's thinking one way or another. Her philosophy *tickled the ears* of women who perceived themselves as being taken advantage of and repressed. In addition, her philosophy helped to intimidate men into sinful passivity in their God-given role as the leader in the family. Unfortunately, it also impacted the church—if not in obviously outward ways, then in subtle but none-the-less unbiblical ways.

In *The Feminine Mystique*, Friedan is obviously searching for some sort of meaning in her life. The words *significance*, *identity*, and *self-actualization* occur over and over. When her book was published in 1963, Friedan was married with three children and said she was frustrated with "exist[ing] only for and through her husband and children."[2] She concluded that her significance came not from her husband but from *her* own identity and *her* own achievements in *her* education and work. (It is important to note that Friedan was wrong in believing that a woman's identity comes from her husband *or* her own achievements. Christians know they are creatures created in God's image, and their identity comes from their relationship with the Lord Jesus Christ.) Spiritually blind and rejecting God as the One who gave purpose to her existence, she was named "Humanist of the Year" in 1975.

After Friedan graduated from college, she studied graduate psychology from psychologist Erik Erikson. Instead of looking to God and His Word for answers, Erikson had studied psychiatry under Sigmund Freud's daughter, Anna. He also had been greatly influenced by the work of avowed atheist Abraham Maslow. Erikson theorized that people go through crisis stages throughout their lives. Those who successfully navigate through each crisis stage develop a healthy, mature personality. Those who do not develop a healthy, mature personality end up with emotional problems. One of Erikson's stages is the adolescent identity crisis.[3] According to Erikson, the adolescent *must* rebel against his parents to find his own identity. (Never mind that the Bible teaches that a person's identity is as a creature of God, made in His image.) Heavily influenced by Erikson as well as other psychologists, Friedan wrote, "In a larger sense this book might never have been written if I had not had a most unusual education in psychology from . . . Erik Erikson at Berkeley. . . ."[4] In *The Feminine Mystique*, Friedan calls Erikson "brilliant."[5]

Borrowing from Erikson's supposed "brilliant" idea, Friedan came up with her own—that a woman's mature identity would not be achieved through marriage and motherhood but through her own achievements in education and career. Here's how Friedan explained the woman's plight:

> By the promise of magical fulfillment through marriage, the *feminine mystique* (that vague, mysterious something that makes women passive and dependant and is tied up with their femininity) arrests their development at an infantile level, short of personal identity. Self-actualizing people [mature, confident people] invariably have a commitment, a sense of mission in life which makes them live in a very large human world, a frame of reference beyond privatism and preoccupation with the petty details of life.[6]

In other words, women who stay home and care for their husbands and families never quite become all they can be. They deal with petty, unimportant areas of life while the men deal with the world and important things. Women, therefore, do not really have their own identity. They are not significant because they do not do anything significant. Their development has been arrested at a child-like state.

Having her own special identity is the heartbeat of Friedan's book. Those who embrace her philosophy often see themselves as victims of our male-dominated society. Friedan believed women are a "target and a victim of the sexual sell."[7] Of course no one would want to be so foolish as to be a victim if they did not have to be. So, Friedan's message is naturally appealing to our sense of, "Yes! I deserve better than this!"

Friedan campaigned for equal pay for equal work and for women to be admitted into every college and every profession. Certainly not everything she desired was wrong, but her underlying philosophy that a woman's identity comes only from her education and/or career was off base and unbiblical. Thus, it fanned the flames of rebellion in women's hearts.

In the 1970s, women began to attend consciousness-raising groups. These groups were intended to be therapeutic through encouraging women to express their frustration and anger about being used by the entire family. The belief was that men and women must be equal in authority, and men must equally share in childcare and housework. A woman must stand up for her rights!

Clearly, it is considered a virtue within the feminist movement *not* to let a man dominate a woman. Well, time passed and the feminist rhetoric cranked up. What Betty Friedan wanted was equal pay and equal rights to an education and a career so that women could achieve their own identities. What feminists want now is acceptance of abortion and homosexuality. In 1992, feminist Marilyn French wrote a book entitled *The War against Women*. In her book, French inflames her readers with statements such as: "Women are being denied human dignity. . . . She is a non-person. . . . A second class citizen. . . . Something is missing in their lives. . . . Wasting their lives by staying home. . . . Marriage has the same effect as the institution of slavery. . . . Breeder-servanthood, a position of subhuman inferiors."[8]

Well, who would want to be a "subhuman inferior"? Certainly not me! So let's look a little closer at French's basis for her conclusions. She blames the pitiful plight of women on (what else?) a male conspiracy to rewrite the Bible and then use it to make women subservient to them:

> The Bible was compiled in a period when patriarchy was spreading, and its editors altered early materials to eradicate signs of an earlier female dominance and to make male supremacy a divine principle. Like the *Iliad* and the *Aeneid*, the Old Testament is great literature that stresses war, male dominance, and murder (of enemies more than compassion or tolerance). If it is God-given and without error, then its values, also God-given, are eternally right. Conservative evangelical Protestants use an inerrant Bible as a major weapon in their war to retain the separate spheres that guarantee male dominance. Women are not immune to the fundamentalist message, and the extreme right often places them in visible positions, usually in movements aimed at impeding or revoking women's rights.[9]

Rejecting the Scriptures as true and God-breathed, French (as well as others) has rewritten history. Without providing proof of her male conspiracy theory, she states it as fact. As far-fetched as this may seem to the reasonable person, the resulting fallout from the feminist belief system has affected much of the world, including Bible believing Christians. For example, Christian women might use "ammunition" from the feminist philosophy to intimidate their husbands and/or pastors to keep the men from being assertive or self-confident. This ploy is confusing and intimidating for men because, just as a woman doesn't want to be a "sub-human inferior," so a man doesn't want to be a "male chauvinist pig!"

How We Have Been Influenced

Because influences are often very subtle, our challenge is to understand how we have been influenced and how we must change. Women do not have to be in full-blown rebellion against men or card-carrying members of the National Organization for Women to have been influenced by this philosophy. Most of us have been influenced even if we are committed Christians. Some of the feminist beliefs that were shocking in the beauty parlors of the 1960s have gradually become accepted in our way of life. The influences may seem subtle and perhaps unimportant, but to the degree that they result in an unbiblical value system, they are deceptive and sinful. Only the Scriptures can guide us through the confusing maze of the influence of feminist thinking.

Conclusion

Figure 9.1 contains only a sampling of how Christians must learn to think through issues by viewing them from God's perspective. It is not a matter of "if" we have been influenced, but "how much" our ears have been tickled to think in terms of what feminist philosophy dictates. Like water to a fish is feminism to the world in which we live! It's all around us. Remember, for

Fig. 9.1 How Feminism Has Influenced Us

Feminist Belief	How We Have Been Influenced	How Scripture Tells Us We Are to Change
"The feminine mystique permits, even encourages, women to ignore the question of their own identity. The mystique says that they can answer the question 'Who am I?' by saying, 'I am [only] Tom's wife. . . .' "[1]	God has gifted me to teach and possibly even preach. It's "who I am." Because he won't let me teach or preach to men, I think my pastor suppresses women with the narrow views he has on their roles. He uses the Bible to back up his teaching but after all, this is the twenty-first century!	When I ask, "Who am I?" the answer is: a woman created by God in His image. My responsibility as God's creature is to glorify Him and serve Him as He desires. This is often in the biblical role of wife and mother. Whether I ever marry or not, I am to use the spiritual gifts God has given me and use them within the Scriptural role of a woman.
"We can no longer ignore that voice within women that says, 'I want something more than my husband and my children and my home.' "[2]	There's got to be more to life than cleaning house. I'm going to do something for myself! My family will survive.	Counter this wrong philosophy by turning your focus from yourself to a desire to honor God (Rom. 12:2) and obey His Word. For example, "I'm going to 'do my work heartily, as for the Lord' and I am choosing to consider my family as more important than myself " (Col. 3:23; Phil. 2:3).
"It is my thesis that the Victorian culture did not permit women to accept or gratify their basic need to grow and fulfill their potentialities as human beings, a *need* which is not solely defined by their sexual role [as a wife and mother]."[3]	What about me? What about my needs? What about my rights? There is something missing in my life. I need my space.	Understand that the "needs" theory is unbiblical. It is unnecessary, unsettling, and unbiblical to think in these terms. Scripture tells us that God has given us *everything we need* "pertaining to life and godliness" (2 Peter 1:3). So, we should be thinking in terms of loving God and loving others and not in terms of our own needs (see Matt. 22:37–40; Titus 2:4).
"Many psychologists, including Freud, have made the mistake of assuming from observations of women who did not have the education and the freedom to play their full part in the world, that it was woman's essential nature to be passive, conformist, dependent, fearful, childlike. . . ."[4]	Women are not inferior to men. I have just as much right to my opinion and way as he does.	There is no partiality with God—whether we are male or female (see Gal. 3:28). Scripture is clear that women are not inferior to men; however, that does not mean I always have a right to express or demand my opinion. My responsibility is to be under my husband's authority (see 1 Cor. 11:3). God knows better than anyone how I can best glorify Him.
"Marriage has the same effect as slavery. . . ."[5]	Biblical submission of a wife to her husband is an outdated concept. Today, the emphasis in the church is on mutual submission.	Being submissive to my husband, unless he asks me to sin, is a primary way that I can serve the Lord Jesus. This attitude may not be popular today, but this is how God has chosen for me to glorify Him. It is a privilege to serve the Lord however He chooses. I am going to pray that my submission will shine as a light in a dark world (see Eph. 5:22–24).

1. Friedan, *The Feminine Mystique*, 71.   2. Ibid., 32.   3. Ibid., 326.   4. Ibid
5. French, *The War against Women*, 181.

Feminist Belief	How We Have Been Influenced	How Scripture Tells Us We Are to Change
"Perhaps it is only a sick or immature society that chooses to make women 'housewives,' not people. Perhaps it is only sick or immature men and women, unwilling to face the great challenges of society, who can retreat for long, without unbearable distress, into that thing-ridden house and make it the end of life itself."[6]	I deserve better than this!	Instead of dwelling on what I think I deserve, I should be thinking that I am to serve the Lord graciously, however He chooses. Part, but not all, of how I am to serve the Lord is by taking care of my family. What a privilege it is to spend my days training my children and caring for our greatest earthly asset, our house.
"Who knows of the possibilities of love [that marriage will be better] when men and women share not only children, home, and garden, not only the fulfillment of their biological roles, but the responsibilities and passions of the work that creates the human future and the full human knowledge of who they are?"[7]	It's not fair that my husband doesn't do half the work around here. If he loved me, he would divide the home responsibilities fifty-fifty.	Lord, let my desire be more to please You (and You have Your way in my life) than to rebel against You by demanding my supposed "equal" rights. Give me a heart to be a joyful worker at home (see Titus 2:5).
"The feminine mystique has succeeded in burying millions of American women alive. There is no way for these women to break out of their comfortable concentration camps except by finally putting forth an effort . . . to help shape the future. Only by such a personal commitment to the future can American women break out of the housewife trap and truly find fulfillment as wives and mothers—by fulfilling their own unique possibilities as separate human beings."[8]	I have been asked to become the director of the pregnancy center. What a wonderful opportunity to serve the Lord! Even though my husband does not want me to, I believe God is calling me to this ministry. I must obey God rather than man!	If God wants me to be the director of the pregnancy center, He will change my husband's heart (without me badgering or nagging him). It is more important that I be holy before the Lord by submitting graciously to my husband's authority than it is that I become director of the pregnancy center (see Eph. 5:22).
"Women, as well as men, can only find their identity in work that uses their full capacities."[9]	Can you believe that our pastor won't let my girlfriend teach the couples Sunday school class? How ridiculous! She is the best teacher in the entire church!	According to the Scriptures, women are not to "teach or exercise authority over a man" (see 1 Tim. 2:12–14). Even though my friend is a great teacher, my pastor is right. I need to support his decision.

6. Friedan, *The Feminine Mystique*, 232.   7. Ibid., 378.   8. Ibid., 336-37.   9. Ibid., 336.

feminists, basically it is all about "me"—my needs, my significance, my rights, my worth, my full development, and my identity. Many have justified feminist beliefs by rewriting history to support the male conspiracy theory. Ironically, feminism has become the conspiracy.

As we study the Scriptures and mature in our understanding of godly thinking and beliefs, we will become more discerning about the wrong ways we have been influenced. Instead of being drawn to the ear-tickling allure of feminist philosophy, the author of Hebrews wrote that our senses will be "trained to discern good and evil" (Heb. 5:14).

God commands all Christians to:

See to it that no one takes you captive through philosophy and empty deception, according to the tradition of men, according to the elementary principles of the world, rather than according to Christ. (Col. 2:8)

The only way we will not be taken captive by the feminist beliefs is through the power of the Holy Spirit and God's grace enabling us to study and believe and embrace what God has told us in His Word. What God has told us in His Word is that women are not victims. We are creatures created in God's image for the purpose of proclaiming His excellencies (1 Peter 2:9).

God, not man, determined how best and in what role women were to give Him glory. It is a joy and a privilege to serve God, but we can do it rightly only on His terms. Feminist beliefs took the world by storm in the 1960s, and feminists have greatly cranked up their rhetoric in recent years. When compared to the eternal Word of God whose flower will never fade (see Isa. 40:8), we see that one of the problems that women face today is the feminist influence.

Another problem that Christian women face today is that of their role within the church. As we will see in the next chapter, the demand for equality does not stop when one enters through the door of the church.

Study Questions

1. How does Betty Friedan's feminist philosophy *tickle the ears* of women?

2. Who is the psychologist that greatly influenced Betty Friedan's thinking? What did he believe?

3. What is the *feminine mystique*? According to the quote on page 137, what does it arrest?

4. What did the feminists in Friedan's day want to achieve? What do the feminists today want to achieve?

5. On what does Marilyn French blame the pitiful plight of women?

6. Read through figure 9.1 and list the ways you think you may have personally been influenced to think wrongly. For each one you list, write out how Scripture tells you to change.

7. What does Colossians 2:8 tell us we are *not* to be taken captive by? What *are* we to be taken captive by?

8. What is your prayer?

10

You Want Me to Do *What?*

The Role of Women in the Church

God is our *Creator*. We are His *creatures*. This is a wonderfully simple but profound concept. This idea is taught very clearly throughout Scripture. It is the reason we exist, and it gives our life meaning and purpose. I remember as a child in public grade school being given the assignment of memorizing Psalm 100. Because of my unbelieving heart, it may as well have been just another poem. Since becoming a Christian, though, the words of this beloved psalm, have taken on a new depth of meaning: "Know that the LORD Himself is God; It is He who has made us, and not we ourselves . . ." (Ps. 100:3).

As a new Christian, there were occasions when I wondered what God was doing, and sometimes it troubled me. It troubled me, that is, until I found Romans 9:

You will say to me then, "Why does He still find fault? For who resists His will?" On the contrary, who are you, O man, who answers back to God? The thing molded will not say to the molder, "Why did you make me like

145

this," will it? Or does not the potter have a right over the clay, to make from the same lump one vessel for honorable use and another for common use? (Rom. 9:19–21)

God's authority over His creatures is clear. He is the potter, and we are His clay. He is our Master, and we are to serve Him as He pleases. He has revealed what He wants us to know and do through His Word, and whatever happens, we are assured that His will for us is good and acceptable and perfect. So instead of reacting to His Word with, "You want me to do *what?*" our obligation is to bow humbly before Him and, as the psalmist wrote, "serve the LORD with gladness" (Ps. 100:2). It is only through understanding and keeping in mind God's authority over us that we can consider the specific biblical ways that women are privileged to serve Him.

Ways Women Are to Serve God

Serving God *begins* with the foundation of being born again and *results* in the ultimate goal of "*proclaim[ing] the excellencies of Him*" (1 Peter 2:9). Look over figure 10.1, beginning at the bottom and moving to the top. Then we will explore each step.

To be *born again* is a supernatural work of God through which He grants saving faith, repentance, and cleansing from sin. When God saves people, He gives them a spiritual rebirth (see 1 Peter 1:3–5). The resulting spiritual life awakens people previously "dead in your trespasses and sins" (Eph. 2:1). As a result, they have a new heart to believe God, to trust Him, and to desire His glory.

The only basis on which God saves sinful man is the Lord Jesus' death on the cross for the punishment of sin. While talking to the religious leader Nicodemus, the Lord Jesus gave him one of the most beloved promises in all of Scripture.

"For God so loved the world, that He gave His only begotten Son, that whoever believes in Him shall not perish, but have eternal life." (John 3:16)

It is only, then, through this God-given foundational process that anyone can begin to mature in his ability to serve the Lord, whatever his role. First, Jesus said, "Truly, truly, I say to you, unless one is born again he cannot see the kingdom of God" (John 3:3).

After a baby is born, he longs for his mother's milk. In much the same way, a newborn Christian longs for the milk of the Word of God (see 1 Peter 2:2). Christian babies grow by studying and retaining Bible doctrine. The more they study, the greater their *general knowledge of doctrine.* (Bible doctrine is simply what the Bible teaches about any particular topic.) So, a Christian needs a basic knowledge of subjects such as the character of God, the Trinity, sin, creation, the gospel, and sanctification (how we grow). It is the Scriptures that are *"profitable for teaching . . .* so that the man of God may be adequate, equipped for every good work" (2 Tim. 3:16–17). A general knowledge of Bible doctrine equips Christians to serve the Lord.

Fig. 10.1 Specific Ways We Are to Serve the Lord

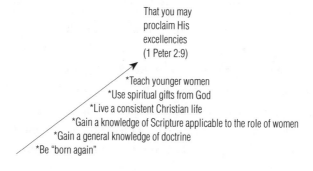

That you may
proclaim His
excellencies
(1 Peter 2:9)

*Teach younger women
*Use spiritual gifts from God
*Live a consistent Christian life
*Gain a knowledge of Scripture applicable to the role of women
*Gain a general knowledge of doctrine
*Be "born again"

Part of being equipped to serve the Lord is to gain a *knowledge of Scripture specifically applicable to the role of women.* Whether it's, "the wife must see to it that she respects her husband," "Your adornment must not be merely external," or "I do not allow a woman to teach or exercise authority over a man," God has given clear guidelines for women to follow concerning their role (Eph. 5:33; 1 Peter 3:3; 1 Tim. 2:12).

Contrary to what some might think, differing roles for men and women are not demeaning for women. They are simply different. Joyously embracing the role God has given you is vital to *living a consistent Christian life.* A woman who is living a consistent Christian life is chaste and pure. She has a desire to please God. She is humble and teachable and not "carried about by every wind of doctrine" (Eph. 4:14). She is consistently and continually growing "in the grace and knowledge of our Lord and Savior Jesus Christ" (2 Peter 3:18).

As a woman lives a consistent Christian life she will also honor God by *using the spiritual gifts* that God has given her (Eph. 4:11–13). Whether teaching, exhorting, serving, or evangelizing, she uses her gifts for the edification of the saints. Her gifts are employed to help others become as much like the Lord Jesus Christ as possible.

As Christian women mature, they become the kind of older women described in Titus 2. They will be "reverent in their behavior, not malicious gossips nor enslaved to much wine, teaching what is good, so that they may encourage the young women . . ." (Titus 2:3–4). There is a special role for the godly older woman to *teach the younger women* "to love their husbands, to love their children, to be sensible, pure, workers at home, kind, being subject to their own husbands . . ." (Titus 2:4–5).

All of the steps along the "Specific Ways to Serve the Lord" figure point to one goal: *"that you may proclaim the excellencies of Him"* (1 Peter 2:9). God's excellencies (such as His holiness, His power, His faithfulness, and His sovereignty) are what make Him superior above His creation. By learning about Him, telling others about Him, and living our lives in ways that bring Him pleasure, we are showing the world that God Most High, truly, is worthy of our goal of bringing honor to Him.

Serving God as He Chooses

The everyday ordinary Christian life is one of great joy and anticipation in what God is doing in us and through us to accomplish His grand design for His creation. It is an incredibly humbling privilege to serve Him in any way that He chooses. Women *are* to use their spiritual gifts and do good works, but they are to use their gifts within the guidelines of God's Word. To better understand these guidelines, let's consider the Scriptures:

Core Scriptures Concerning the Role of Women in the Church

Then God said, "Let Us make man in Our image, according to Our likeness; and let them rule over the fish of the sea and over the birds of the sky and over the cattle and over all the earth, and over every creeping thing that creeps on the earth." (Gen. 1:26)

The triune God is speaking here: "Let *Us* . . . in *Our* image." This is a *general* statement about what God planned to do. In God's plan, they (men and women) were to rule over the creation God prepared for them. This is an overview statement, not a specific treatise spelling out specific roles.

God created man in His own image, in the image of
God He created him; male and female He created them.
(Gen. 1:27)

Again, this is another general statement. More of the specific
details about God creating Adam and Eve are explained in
Genesis 2, but here in chapter 1, God is simply explaining that
He created man (in the sense of all mankind) in His image.
Some people are men and some are women.

In Genesis 2, some of the specific details of the creation of
the first man and the first woman are given. God formed the first
man, Adam, from the dust of the ground. Then God breathed
life into Adam:

Then the LORD God formed man of dust from the
ground, and breathed into his nostrils the breath of life;
and man became a living being. (Gen. 2:7)

Even with all the animals around him, though, there was no
companion for Adam:

Then the LORD God said, "It is not good for the man to
be alone; I will make him a helper suitable for him."
(Gen. 2:18)

So, God took one of Adam's ribs and fashioned the first
woman, Eve. Adam was marvelously delighted, and he named
her "woman." Eve's role was that of "helper suitable" for Adam.
From the very beginning of time, woman was created to be a
helper and companion to her husband. God's original intent was
for Eve to have a different role than Adam. "God made the man
the head and the female the helper. It is God who wants men to

be men and women to be women; and He can teach us the meaning of each, if we want to be taught. . . . Maleness and femaleness identify their roles."[1] God created the man to lead, and the woman to help and follow.

> Now the serpent was more crafty than any beast of the field which the LORD God had made. And he said to the woman, "Indeed, has God said, 'You shall not eat from any tree of the garden'?" The woman said to the serpent, "From the fruit of the trees of the garden we may eat; but from the fruit of the tree which is in the middle of the garden, God has said, 'You shall not eat from it or touch it, or you will die.' " The serpent said to the woman, "You surely will not die! For God knows that in the day you eat from it your eyes will be opened, and you will be like God, knowing good and evil." When the woman saw that the tree was good for food, and that it was a delight to the eyes, and that the tree was desirable to make one wise, she took from its fruit and ate; and she gave also to her husband with her, and he ate. (Gen. 3:1–6)

Eve came to believe that God was keeping something from her. She began to doubt the goodness of God. Just as Satan had desired in his heart to be like God, so did Eve. She rebelled against her Creator. Unlike Eve who was deceived, though, Adam knew full well what he was doing. He followed her into sin, and as he took that step, he dragged us with him. How sad. Because sin is contrary to God's nature, God pronounced a swift and devastating judgment on Satan first, then Adam, and then lastly on Eve:

> To the woman He said,
> "I will greatly multiply

Your pain in childbirth,
In pain you will bring forth children;
Yet your desire will be for your husband,
And he will rule over you." (Gen. 3:16)

Part of God's judgment was addressed specifically to Eve. Her desire would now be to overtake her husband, yet Adam would rule over her. The man's authority over his wife would continue as it had from the beginning, but now it would include a sinful struggle between husband and wife. What once had been a joyful fulfilling of roles became a power play for control. The apostle Paul elaborated on the roles of men and women in 1 Corinthians:

But I want you to understand that Christ is the head of every man, and the man is the head of a woman, and God is the head of Christ. . . . For a man . . . is the image and glory of God; but the woman is the glory of man. For man does not originate from woman, but woman from man; for indeed man was not created for the woman's sake, but woman for the man's sake. . . . However, in the Lord, neither is woman independent of man, nor is man independent of woman. For as the woman originates from the man, so also the man has his birth through the woman; and all things originate from God. (1 Cor. 11:3, 7–9, 11–12)

In this section of Scripture, the apostle Paul makes it clear that the wife is under the authority of her husband, and the husband is under the authority of Christ. The structure of this authority is seen in figure 10.2:

Some believe that the apostle Paul was chauvinistic because of the Roman culture of his day. However, Paul plainly bases his declaration that "the woman was created for the man's sake" on God's *original intent*, not on the way the Romans treated women. Genesis clearly says that the woman was created for the man's sake. This is simply her God-given role, then and now:

> The women are to keep silent in the churches; for they are not permitted to speak, but are to subject themselves just as the Law also says. If they desire to learn anything, let them ask their own husbands at home; for it is improper for a woman to speak in church. (1 Cor. 14:34–35)

Certainly these verses would stir up any latent feminist leanings one might have! Stir them up, that is, to anger. Well, before we get too upset, let's think about what was happening in Corinth. The Corinthian Christians were competing for attention with the "showy" gifts (speaking in tongues and prophecy). Consequently, they were creating chaos and disorder in the churches. Paul wrote that however they used their gifts, the gifts were to be exercised for the edification of other believers, in an orderly manner, with an interpreter, or the people were to keep silent. Concerning women voicing their opinions, women were

Fig. 10.2 Structure of Authority in 1 Corinthians 11

* God
- Christ
  - Man
  - Woman
    - Under the man's headship (v. 3)
    - The glory of man (v. 7)
    - Created for the man's sake (v. 9)

in church to learn rather than to create confusion or to usurp the elder's teaching position. Paul's explanation in 1 Corinthians 14 concerning the role of women in the church is also consistent with what he wrote in 1 Timothy 2:11 (which we will discuss next), and, of course, is consistent with God's original intent, which we clearly saw in Genesis 1–3.

> Likewise, I want women to adorn themselves with proper clothing, modestly and discreetly, not with braided hair and gold or pearls or costly garments, but rather by means of good works, as is proper for women making a claim to godliness. A woman must quietly receive instruction with entire submissiveness. But I do not allow a woman to teach or exercise authority over a man, but to remain quiet. For it was Adam who was first created and then Eve. And it was not Adam who was deceived, but the woman being deceived, fell into transgression. But women will be preserved through the bearing of children if they continue in faith and love and sanctity with self-restraint. (1 Tim. 2:9–15)

In this section of 1 Timothy, Paul again refers back to the creation order ("it was Adam who was first created and then Eve"). All Christian women are daughters of Eve in the sense that we risk being deceived and deceiving others when it comes to teaching Bible doctrine. At least two points are very clear. First, women are not to be in authority over the men in the church. Positions of authority over men would include being a pastor and/or holding a position on the elder or deacon board. Secondly, women are not to teach Bible doctrine to men. This would include preaching and teaching Bible studies.

Certainly women may be exceptionally gifted teachers, so how should they use their gift of teaching? The answer is that they are to teach the women, as we see in Titus 2:1–7:

> But as for you, speak the things which are fitting for sound doctrine. Older men are to be temperate, dignified, sensible, sound in faith, in love, in perseverance.
>
> Older women likewise are to be reverent in their behavior, not malicious gossips nor enslaved to much wine, teaching what is good, so that they may encourage the young women to love their husbands, to love their children, to be sensible, pure, workers at home, kind, being subject to their own husbands, so that the word of God will not be dishonored.

Paul wrote this letter to Titus who was overseeing the church on the island of Crete. He gave Titus specific instructions for qualified, mature believers of both sexes and all ages. Among those instructions is this section written for the older women. Titus tells the older women that their characters are to be sterling so that they will not dishonor God's Word. They were *not to be* gossips or drunkards, but they *were to be* godly in their behavior, as well as teachers and encouragers of the young women.

The women in these churches were not at all considered to be second-class citizens. In fact, if they were really godly, they had a responsibility to pour their lives into the lives of the younger women. Raising a family was not the end of the wife and mother's obligation, but merely a stepping-stone and training ground for the second phase of a woman's ministry—teaching younger women.

In addition to the outward behavior godly women are to have, they are also to have an unfading inward adornment:

In the same way, you wives, be submissive to your own husbands so that even if any of them are disobedient to the word, they may be won without a word by the behavior of their wives, as they observe your chaste and respectful behavior. Your adornment must not be merely external—braiding the hair, and wearing gold jewelry, or putting on dresses; but let it be the hidden person of the heart, with the imperishable quality of a gentle and quiet spirit, which is precious in the sight of God. For in this way in former times the holy women also, who hoped in God, used to adorn themselves, being submissive to their own husbands; just as Sarah obeyed Abraham, calling him lord, and you have become her children if you do what is right without being frightened by any fear. (1 Peter 3:1–6)

The apostle Peter tells wives and women that true beauty is a gentle and quiet spirit. A woman with a gentle and quiet spirit is not given to fear or anger. Neither does she contend or dispute with God. Instead, she accepts God's dealings with her as good. In addition to having a gentle and quiet spirit, Peter exhorts his original readers, and us, to be like the holy women of old who hoped in God by doing "what is right without being frightened by any fear."

Now that we have looked at specific ways women are to serve the Lord and have considered Scriptures concerning the role of women, let's think about how women are restricted in serving.

Ways Women Are Restricted in Serving

As we have already seen, God is the sovereign authority over His creation, and this includes the roles of men and women.

The New Testament Scriptures give additional details of the woman's role that are perfectly consistent with God's original intent. How women are to use their spiritual gifts is God's express will. And we know from Romans 12:2 that God's will is always *"good* and *acceptable* and *perfect."* With that in mind, consider figure 10.3, which depicts the biblical restrictions. Read from the bottom up and keep in mind that the overarching goal is the same as before: "so that you may proclaim the excellencies of Him" (1 Peter 2:9).

When we compare these restrictions with the previous diagram (Fig. 10.1) of how women are to serve, it seems that there is so much women are to be doing that our restrictions pale in comparison. We should not seek to teach and have positions of authority over the men in the church, but we should have great joy in how God uses us. After all, why should we seek to have preeminence or even equality when we have the example of our Lord Jesus submitting Himself to the will of the Father (see Phil. 2:5–8)?

A woman's ministry in the church is an extension of her ministry in the home and in her community. God's original intent has not changed nor will it ever change. Of course, there have

Fig. 10.3 What God Ordains

That you may
proclaim His
excellencies
(1 Peter 2:9)

*Be glad you do not have to bear the burdens the elders bear (Heb. 13:17)
*Be content in the role God has given you (1 Peter 3:1–6)
*Not teach men (1 Tim. 2:12)
*Not usurp the men's authority (1 Tim. 2:12)
*Not disrupt the church service with questions or contention (1 Cor. 14:34–35)
*Graciously submit to and defer to the elders in the church (Heb. 13:17)

been many times when men have sinfully taken advantage of women, but I believe that Scripture has provided biblical means to protect women. In the circumstances where a woman does suffer because of a man sinfully lording (his authority) over her, she (in a very small way like her Lord) will be suffering for righteousness sake (see Matt. 5:10–12).[2]

Conclusion

Satan sought to usurp God's authority. Eve did usurp God's and Adam's authority, but we do not have to be like them. For those who are in Christ, we have His supernatural grace to be grateful for, have joy in, and be content in the role He has given us. For all that we are restricted in doing, there is ever so much more that we should be doing. We should be as *good as possible* in the tasks and responsibilities that God has given us. It seems to me that instead of contending with God over the matter of a woman's role and asking, "You want me to do *what*?" we should be grateful to Him for giving us life and defining our role. We should serve Him joyfully and look to the Scriptures for God's clearly defined intent of how women are to pattern their lives. Christian women are to use their spiritual gifts, but we are to use them as God intended. After all, God is our Creator.

⟨⟨⟨⟨⟨⟨ *Study Questions* ⟩⟩⟩⟩⟩⟩

1. According to the introductory paragraphs in this chapter, what is our obligation to God?

2. List the steps (from bottom to top) of specific ways we *are* to serve the Lord. For each step give one Scripture reference.

3. What does it mean to proclaim God's excellencies? See 1 Peter 2:9.

4. Describe the ordinary Christian life (see page 149).

5. Match the following:

A general statement about what God planned to do when He created mankind.	Genesis 2:18
A specific statement about God creating Adam.	Genesis 3:1–6
The reason why God created Eve.	Genesis 2:7
The incident that resulted in Eve believing God was keeping something from her.	Genesis 3:16
God's judgment on Eve.	Genesis 1:26

6. According to 1 Corinthians 11:3–16, why was woman created?

7. According to 1 Timothy 2:9–15, how is a godly woman adorned? Why does Paul say women are not to teach or exercise authority over the men in the church?

8. Which Scripture makes it clear what the older women are to teach the younger women?

9. What does it mean to have a "gentle and quiet spirit"? See 1 Peter 3:1–7.

10. List the four ways women are restricted in serving in the church (hint: see the bottom four on the "What God Ordains" chart).

11. According to the "What God Ordains" chart, what are the responsibilities of women in the church?

12. How have you been influenced to think wrongly about your role as a Christian woman in the church? How should you change?

11

Be Thankful?
You Can't Be Serious!

TRIALS

"Why me?" "Why doesn't God do something?" "Why is God letting this happen to us?" "Why does God let little children die?" "Why did God sit back and not stop the slaughter of Jews in Nazi Germany or the death of three thousand innocent people on 9/11 in New York City?" "Why . . . ?" "Why . . . ?" "Why . . . ?"

The "Why?" question is common as people grapple with trials. Although it is possible to have an innocent motive in asking the "Why?" question, most people ask "Why?" because they are upset with God. Some conclude that there must not be a God. Others believe there is a God, but He must be powerless to prevent trials. Still others preach and teach that we have to come to the place where we forgive God.

All of these conclusions have one thing in common—they are blasphemous. They malign God's character by accusing Him of not being good. Of the many women I have counseled, there have been some who were in extremely difficult circumstances,

161

but in spite of their circumstances, they were grateful to God for what He was doing and how He was helping them. Their trials were catastrophic yet they were experiencing the peace of God. On the other hand, some ladies were angry and emotionally disturbed. But their emotional pain was far beyond the bounds of what would be expected in their very tiny trial. Fueling this second group of women were two beliefs: they were not persuaded of the goodness of God, and they were not grateful to Him. Instead of God's peace, they experienced frustration and fear and bitterness. Desperate for relief from their emotional pain, they did not give God glory. Instead, they blamed Him.

To make some sense out of the tests and trials that we all experience, let's consider three biblical principles that teach us about God and what He is doing in our lives.

God's Purposes and Our Tests

The first principle is that God is sovereign. "But our God is in the heavens; He does whatever He pleases" (Ps. 115:3). Like the potter molds the clay, God created us and therefore has authority over us whether we like it or not. He is the highest authority, and He actively rules over His creatures and all of His creation. For instance, His sovereign hand is over the weather as well as a traffic light that isn't working. Scripture also teaches us that we (His creatures) were created for God's "glory" (Isa. 43:7). Therefore, in order to glorify him, we are to submit ourselves to His sovereign hand.

This leads us to the second principle. God decided (decreed) how we may best give Him glory. The only way to give God glory is to become more and more like Him. God uses the circumstances in our lives to test us and mold us into his image. It is clear from the Scriptures that "those whom He foreknew, He also predestined to become conformed to the image of His Son" (Rom. 8:29). In fact, there is nothing that happens to us by chance or in vain. "God causes *all* things to work together for good to those who love God . . ." (Rom. 8:28).

"All things" includes blessings such as the abilities He gives us, our family and friends, or a beautiful sunset. Our life and every breath we take is also a blessing. Saving us is the most astounding blessing of all. Our salvation showcases His mercy, His holiness, His worth, and our utter inability to save ourselves (Eph. 2:8–9).

In addition to blessings, "all things" also includes sin. God is not the author of sin, we are; but He does permit others to sin against us, and He does use it for His purposes. Joseph drove home this point when he told his brothers, "You meant evil against me but God meant it for good . . ." (Gen. 50:20).

Another way that God causes "all things" to work together for our good is when He channels the king's heart (Prov. 21:1). He hardens hearts as well as softens hearts. So whether it was Pharaoh's hard heart that wouldn't let the Jews out of their slavery in Egypt or a previous Pharaoh's soft heart that *did* let Joseph out of prison and made him a ruler over Egypt, God works in His creation to bring about His ultimate purpose—His glory. As a by-product of His glory, believers have been given new hearts that are capable of proclaiming His excellencies regardless of their circumstances.

The third principle is that God sometimes tests us, and when He does, He has a definite purpose or purposes. The test may be the unexpected death of a loved one or a long, difficult illness for yourself. Maybe your child has a temper tantrum for all the grocery store to see and hear! Husbands leave their wives for other women. People are mugged walking down the street. We know these tests are for His glory and our good, but what more can we know of His purposes for the trials in our life?

One purpose God may have for putting us through a trial is to prune us so that we may bear more fruit for His glory. In John 15, the Lord Jesus likens Himself to the vine and us to the branches. God the Father is the husbandman who cuts dead branches off and prunes back live branches for the purpose of the branch bearing more fruit. I would think that if a plant or a tree could feel pain, having a branch chopped off would be agonizingly painful. Eventually, though, the pain would be forgotten as the branch produced beautifully flowering buds soon to turn into fruit. For those who abide in His Word, a similar pruning will most certainly take place. Sometimes that pruning is precipitated by a trial. Trials often bring out the worst in us: anger, bitterness, fear, laziness, self-focus, etc. But thankfully, this "worst" is pruned off as God convicts us of our sin and helps us turn from sin to righteousness. The pain from God's pruning will fade as the fruit of righteousness flowers for all to see.

A second purpose God may have in testing us is to discipline us for our good. I think this is akin to being pruned. Being disciplined hurts and is embarrassing. Fortunately for us, God has a pure motive and a compassionate heart. He disciplines those whom He loves. As a result, He will not let us continue indefinitely in our sin. You see, He wants us to "share His holiness" (Heb. 12:10). Hebrews 12 explains that, like pruning, discipline "for the moment seems not to be joyful, but sorrowful" but, also like pruning, "afterwards it yields the peaceful fruit of righteousness" (Heb. 12:11). If you undergo a trial as a consequence of your own sin, God will discipline you—whether the result is spending time in jail or experiencing emotional turmoil. He will do whatever it takes for you to give Him glory.

In addition to being pruned and disciplined by tests and trials, God gives us special opportunities to see if our faith is proven to be genuine (see 1 Peter 1:7). It is easy to act like a Christian and be charitable toward others when things are going our way, but how easy is it when you are being laughed at because of your faith or traumatized because your house has just burned to the ground? All trials, however great or small, give us an "on the spot" opportunity to prove who we *really* worship and serve—our own comfort or our Lord? The apostle Peter wrote to Christians warning them to prepare for persecution, and he prayed that the testing of their faith would *prove* to be found genuine and *result* in praise, glory, and honor to God (see 1 Peter 1:7).

God uses all of these purposes for trials (pruning, discipline, and testing our faith) to mature us. In fact, James wrote to Christians to:

> Consider it all joy, my brethren, when you encounter various trials, knowing that the testing of your faith produces endurance. And let endurance have its perfect result, so that you may be perfect and complete, lacking in nothing. (James 1:2–4)

Since God has revealed through Scripture some of His high and holy purposes for trying and testing us, what, then, is our obligation? Our obligation is to be grateful to God, to be fully persuaded of His goodness, and to realize how much He loves us.

A person who is grateful to God is always giving thanks in everything (see 1 Thess. 5:18). Being thankful is similar to loving someone. Sometimes you *feel* as if you love the other person, but sometimes you *show* love regardless of how you feel. Gratitude to God is either a thought or an action. It may or may not include a wonderful feeling of gratitude. Regardless of how you feel, God's command is clear:

Let the peace of Christ rule in your hearts, to which indeed you were called in one body; and *be thankful*. Let the word of Christ richly dwell within you, with all wisdom teaching and admonishing one another with psalms and hymns and spiritual songs, *singing with thankfulness* in your hearts to God. Whatever you do in word or deed, do all in the name of the Lord Jesus, *giving thanks through Him* to God the Father. (Col. 3:15–17)

When our church was new and our congregation small, there was no one who could play the piano but me. That was tough for me because playing the piano is not exactly my greatest gift. In spite of that, I was the designated pianist. The Lord taught me a lot about humility during that time, but one particular Sunday stands out vividly in my mind—it was our first Sunday renting space in a local school. I was looking forward to that Sunday because I thought their piano was better than our previous one. It took only one note to find out otherwise. The keys were uneven, it was grossly out of tune, and it sounded like a honky-tonk bar piano. As the minister of music and I practiced before Sunday school, I thought, *Lord, why? Why can't we have a half-way decent piano? The church on the corner doesn't even believe your Word is true, and they have a seven-foot Steinway!*

As I struggled in my thoughts about what God was doing, I began to cry. Jerry Gunter, our music minister, could not help but notice. He stopped singing and came over beside the piano. He said, "I think we need to pray." Through my tears, I nodded. His prayer went something like this, "Lord, *thank You* for this piano." I was dumbfounded, and if that wasn't bad enough he added, "And I pray that Martha will repent of her pride." I did not repent right then, but I did quit crying. Later, instead of listening to the Sunday school lesson, I continued to struggle in my thoughts with the Lord. Finally, I realized my sin, and with a contrite heart I thought, *Lord, forgive me for being angry about the piano. Thank You for the piano and for testing me.*

I had been caught off guard by this rather insignificant little test, and I failed miserably. As miserable as it felt, though, God was teaching me that I am to be thankful *always*, no matter what happens to me or to a loved one. If my first thought had been, *I am to be thankful for all things. Thank you, Lord, for this piano,* God would have been glorified instead of being made the villain. I would not have *felt* great happiness, but I would have had joy in God's purposes.

In addition to being grateful, another obligation we have is to be fully persuaded of God's goodness:

> Shout joyfully to the LORD, all the earth.
> Serve the LORD with gladness;
> Come before Him with joyful singing.
> Know that the LORD Himself is God;
> It is He who has made us, and not we ourselves;
> We are His people and the sheep of His pasture.
>
> Enter His courts with thanksgiving
> And His courts with praise.
> Give thanks to Him, bless His name.
> For the LORD is good;
> His lovingkindness is everlasting
> And His faithfulness to all generations. (Ps. 100)

Suppose you receive an unexpected bad report on your mammogram. Or you learn of the sudden death of a loved one. Or you find out your child's spouse is leaving him or her. At the very least, your emotions will be reeling. You probably will not be able to sleep. Grief will wash over you like a wave at the beach. While all of these are trying times, you must remind yourself of the goodness of God. Pray and think, "Lord, You are good to have let me live this long with clear mammograms." Or "You are good to have let me have my loved one for as long as I did." Or "You are good to our child because he or she does not have to go through this marriage separation in vain."

You should also remind yourself that God is good regardless of your circumstances. A person who loves Him will be convinced of God's goodness on days sprinkled with small aggravating tests as well as on days consumed by immense, grievous trials. God is good, and good thoughts of Him should fill our hearts always.

A third obligation we have is to realize that God must love us very much to test our faith as He does. We know that God has set a special love toward His children. His love is everlasting. It is eternal (Ps. 136). He also sets the supreme high and holy standard for love: "In this is love, not that we loved God, but that He loved us and sent His son to be the propitiation for our sins" (1 John 4:10). As mentioned before, He even disciplines us in love: "For those whom the Lord loves He disciplines" (Heb. 12:6). As a matter of fact, God cannot have decreed any test or trial for us that is not motivated by love.

Several years ago I heard about a tragic automobile accident in which two young men who had recently graduated from The Master's Seminary were hit by a drunk driver and killed. They were good friends and had planned to go to France to the mission field along with their families. Both were married, and one had four very small children. Our church grieved their loss and prayed for the Stride family and the Saunders family. Not long after, I received a phone call from a friend of one of the wives. Her friend asked me if I would write to Lois Stride, and I agreed. As I thought about and struggled with what to say, I expressed our sympathy and told her that our entire church was praying for her and her children, and I concluded my note with something like this:

> I won't pretend to know why this has happened but I do know one thing—God must love you very much to test your faith at this level. My prayer for you is that your faith will be proven to be genuine.

Much later I heard through the "Christian grapevine" that God had used what I wrote to comfort Lois and to strengthen her during her grief. Lois was comforted by the fact that God loved her and that He had His own supreme purposes behind the agonizing test of her faith.[1]

Conclusion

It is a grand and glorious mystery how God sovereignly works in His creation. He has decreed from eternity past how we may best give Him glory. He has very definite and good purposes for us as He tests us. Our obligation is to be grateful, to be fully persuaded of His goodness, and to realize how much He loves us. Then we can face whatever test or trial comes upon us, knowing that God is working in our life and the lives of our loved ones to accomplish His divine purposes.

❧❧❧❧❧❧❧ *Study Questions* ❧❧❧❧❧❧❧

1. What are two wrong beliefs about God?
2. Fill in the blanks: "But our God is in the _____; He does whatever He _____" (Ps. 115:3).

3. What do we learn from Romans 8:28–29 about God's purpose in our trials?

4. What is God's overriding purpose as He works in His creation?

5. Match the following:

The branches are pruned so they may bear more fruit.	James 1:2–4
God disciplines us so that we may share His holiness.	1 Peter 1:7
Trials test our faith so we may praise and honor God more.	John 15:2
Testing our faith produces endurance.	Hebrews 12:10

6. How is being thankful similar to loving someone? See page 165.

7. Fill in the blanks from 1 Thessalonians 5:18: "In _____ give _____; for this is God's _____ for _____ in Christ Jesus." Now repeat this verse aloud over and over until you can say it by memory.

8. According to page 167, what is our second obligation before God?

9. Honoring God by being persuaded of God's goodness will not happen automatically in a severe trial. It begins with thinking correctly in the little tests each and every day. Write out three examples of a test and how to respond acknowledging God's goodness.

10. What is our third obligation to realize when we face a trial? See page 168.

11. Realizing that you may have to face one or more trials in your life, what is your prayer now?

Conclusion

This book began on a warm, sunny day in Peachtree City, Georgia. It ends on a cold, blustery day between Christmas and New Year's Day. As I think about the hundreds of women that I have had the privilege to counsel using the Scriptures, there are a number of problems that women face. Certainly, this book did not cover all the problems women have, but by God's grace, it did cover some of them.

In chapters 2–5, we considered problems that women have with others. We learned that gossip and slander are vicious, ugly sins, and we all know that the tongue is hard to tame! Another problem with others is idolatrous emotional attachments that occur when there is homosexuality or heterosexual promiscuity. The emotions are inordinate and difficult to overcome, but by God's grace it is possible to break those bonds and have a pure heart.

Another very common problem with others is manipulation. We must learn not to answer back like a fool but give those acting like fools the answer they deserve so that they won't be wise in their own eyes. And the last problem we considered in this section was hurt feelings. We basically concluded that we shouldn't really be thinking in terms of our "hurt feelings." Rather, we should be thinking in terms of loving God and loving the other person who hurt us.

The second section that we covered was "Problems with Ourselves." Chapter 6 uncovered vanity as an especially grotesque sin. Chapter 7 explained the PMS mess, and we learned that hormones are no excuse to go berserk. In addition, we saw several practical tips to make that time of month more bearable. The last chapter in this section covered the problem of legalism. Legalism crowds out love for the brethren, and so it creates disdain for others. We all have to be on guard not to fall into the trap of the Pharisees.

The feminist influence and the role of women in the church have created a firestorm of controversy in the church. Chapters 9–11 were meant to calm that storm and replace it with a heart of joy for the woman serving her Lord however He ordains.

⁂

When I was young, women had problems. Now they have "issues." Regardless of what you call them, they are very distressful to the women experiencing them. There are clear, sufficient answers in the Scriptures for the Christian woman. I hope from this study you have gained a clear biblical picture of what your problem is and, by God's grace, the solution.

⁂

May God use this book to richly bless you for His glory.

Appendix:
Salvation Worksheets[1]

Who Is Jesus Christ?

The Bible tells us much about Jesus and who He is. Jesus Himself made many of the claims, and others made many claims about Him. Look up the following references and write down what these claims are. Before you begin your study, say a brief prayer to God and ask Him to show you if these claims are true.

   1. What does Jesus call Himself?
      a. John 4:25–26
      b. John 8:28; 9:35–38
      c. Matthew 27:42–43

"Son of God" and "Son of Man" are Old Testament expressions for the Messiah who was predicted to come. The prophets in the Old Testament knew that this Messiah was God and that He was worthy of worship (see Dan. 7:13–14).

   2. What does Jesus claim about Himself?
      a. John 5:39
      b. John 6:51
      c. John 8:12
      d. John 8:58
      e. John 10:30; 14:7–9

3. The Trinity is three divine persons (God the Father, God the Son, and God the Holy Spirit) who are the same in essence and nature yet have distinct personalities. When God the Son, Jesus, lived here on earth for thirty-three years, He subordinated himself to the will of God the Father. Why? See Philippians 2:5–8.

4. The apostle Paul says in his letter to Titus that God is our Savior (Titus 1:3).
    a. Whom does Paul then say our Savior is (Titus 1:3–4)?
    b. What else does Paul say about Jesus (Col. 1:15–16)?

5. Whom did Peter say that Jesus was?
    a. Mark 8:27–29
    b. 2 Peter 1:1

6. Whom did John the Baptist say that Jesus was (John 1:29, 34)?

7. Whom did the apostle John say Jesus was?
    a. John 1:1, 14
    b. Revelation 19:16

8. Whom did God the Father say Jesus was (Matt. 3:17)?

9. Who has the authority to forgive sins?
    a. Luke 5:21
    b. Who forgave the paralytic's sins (Luke 5:17–20)?
    c. What did Jesus do to prove that He had authority to forgive sins (Luke 5:21–24)?

Summary
Jesus claimed to be God by saying He:
- was the "Son of God"
- was the "Son of Man"

Appendix   175

- was the Savior (the Messiah)
- had authority to forgive sins

Jesus proved that He was God by:

- the works that He did (for example, Creation)
- the miracles that He did
- His resurrection from the dead

The teaching of the Bible that Jesus is God is not something that we can explain by human logic. It is a supernatural truth that we believe because God's Spirit illumines the truth to us.

What Jesus Did on the Cross

Just about everyone in America has heard of Jesus and knows that He died on the cross. However, they may have many misconceptions about the purpose of His death.

1. How was Jesus killed (Matt. 27:35)?

2. What did the sign over His head say (Mark 15:26)?

3. What did the people say who were making fun of Jesus (Luke 23:35–37)?

4. How did the soldiers decide to divide up Jesus' garments (John 19:24)?

5. Which four books in the Bible contain the story of Jesus' death on the cross?

6. Make a list of what Jesus said as He was on the cross:
   a. Luke 23:34
   b. Luke 23:42–43
   c. Luke 23:46
   d. John 19:25–26

    e. John 19:30

    f. Mark 15:37–38

7. What was the purpose of Jesus' death?

    a. 1 Peter 2:24

    b. Hebrews 2:17 ("propitiation" means to satisfy God's wrath)

    c. Ephesians 1:7 ("In Him" refers back to Jesus Christ)

    d. Romans 4:25 ("He" refers back to Jesus)

    e. Romans 5:9

    f. 1 Corinthians 15:3

Jesus told His disciples that the "Scriptures" (the Old Testament) were about Him (John 5:39). Indeed, there are many places in the Old Testament that foretell of the coming Messiah and what He would do for the people so that they could be reconciled to God. (Sin had put a barrier between people and God because God is holy.) Jesus' death on the cross was God's way of punishing sin so that God's sense of justice could be satisfied. In other words, Jesus was punished in our place.

One of the most detailed descriptions of how Jesus took our punishment is in Isaiah 53. Isaiah wrote this over seven hundred years before Jesus was born. God gave this information to Isaiah supernaturally; Isaiah doesn't call Jesus by His name but calls him the "Servant."

8. How was Jesus treated by men (Isa. 53:3)?

9. What did He bear for us (Isa. 53:4)?

10. What happened to Jesus because of our "transgressions" (our sins) and our "iniquities" (our sins; Isa. 53:5)?

11. Isaiah 53:5 says, "The chastening (punishment that we deserve) for our _____ fell upon Him."

12. Isaiah 53:6 says, "But the LORD has caused the iniquity [sin] of us all to _____"

13. What kind of sacrificial offering was Jesus (Isa. 53:10)?

14. Where was Jesus' anguish (Isa. 53:11)?

15. What will He bear (Isa. 53:11)?

16. Isaiah 53:12 says, "Yet He Himself bore the _____."

17. What was God's motive for sending Jesus to die for our sins (1 John 4:10)?

Summary

Jesus died on the cross to take the punishment for our sins. He died in our place. He paid the full penalty and then He said,

"It is finished!"

What Does the Bible Teach about Sin?

In the last section we studied Jesus' death on the cross and we learned that He died to take the punishment for our sin. Also, we learned that God was satisfied sin had been sufficiently punished and that Jesus' resurrection from the dead is the proof. In this section, we are going to study about sin: who sinned first, why they sinned, and why and how we sin today. Some sins are obvious (murder, for example). Some sins are obvious only to God. Regardless of which kind of sin we commit, all sin grieves God because He is perfectly pure and holy. Therefore, we need to understand just what sin is and how to properly deal with it.

1. The first created being to sin was an angel name Lucifer (later his name became Satan). His problem was pride. He wanted to be worshiped like God was worshiped by some of the other angels. Lucifer made a "power play" in heaven, and God cast Lucifer and all his followers out. What did Lucifer want? See Isaiah 14:13–14. List the five "I will" statements of Lucifer:

     a.

     b.

     c.

     d.

     e.

2. Lucifer had a real problem with pride. He should have been grateful to worship and serve God. Instead, he wanted all the attention himself. What was the underlying reason for thinking he deserved that kind of attention (Ezek. 28:17)?

3. Lucifer was the first angel to sin, and Adam and Eve were the first human beings to sin. When God created Adam and Eve they were innocent and without sin. God put them in the Garden of Eden, which had a perfect environment, and then God tested their devotion to Him; God told them they could eat fruit off any tree except one: "the tree of the knowledge of good and evil." God warned them that if they disobeyed, they would die.

     a. Satan was not content to leave well enough alone. He decided to try to get Adam and Eve to follow him by disobeying God. Satan appeared to Eve in the form of a serpent. See Genesis 3:1.

         1) How is the serpent described?

         2) What did he ask Eve?

     b. God told Eve if she ate from that tree she would die. What did Satan tell her would happen (Gen. 3:4)?

c. Whom did Satan tell Eve she would be like if she ate (Gen. 3:5)?

d. What did Eve decide to do (Gen. 3:6)?

e. Before they sinned, Adam and Eve were very comfortable around God and not afraid of Him. What was their response to God now (Gen. 3:10)?

f. God confronted Adam and Eve with their sin. Whom did Adam blame (Gen. 3:12)?

g. Whom did Eve blame (Gen. 3:13)?

4. Because God is holy, He has to punish sin. He pronounced judgment right then on Satan, Eve, and Adam. What was one part of the punishment (Gen. 3:19)?

5. After Adam and Eve sinned, they knew sin in a personal, experiential way. It had become part of their natural nature and was then passed down to their children and their children's children, etc. Also, the consequences of sin were passed down.

a. Why did "death spread to all men" (Rom. 5:12)?

b. What is the "just" consequence of sin (Rom. 6:23)?

6. The Bible classifies sin by different terms such as transgression, iniquity, wickedness, evil, disobedience, and unbelief. Look up the following verses and list what the particular sin is:

a. Romans 13:1

b. 1 Corinthians 6:18

c. Ephesians 4:25–29 (These sins are obvious sins.)

d. Ephesians 4:31 (These sins may be obvious or may be "mental attitude" sins. Mental attitude sins are sins that we "think," which may or may not result in an additional, obvious sin.)

e. Ephesians 5:18

   f. Philippians 4:6
   g. James 3:6
   h. James 4:17
   i. James 5:12

7. All sin, whether open or hidden, is seen and remembered by God. What does God judge (Heb. 4:12)?

8. Is there anything hidden from God (Heb. 4:13)?

9. God is holy. Therefore, He must punish sin. Man sins. Therefore, man is separated from God and the result is death. However, God loves man. So, He provided a way for man's sins to be punished, and for man to be with Him for all eternity. The way that God provided is Jesus' death on the cross bearing our punishment. How is it that we can know that we, personally, are in a right relationship with God? That *our* sins are taken care of? See Acts 16:31.

10. Oftentimes, people know about Jesus but they are still depending partly on themselves to be good enough to earn their way into heaven. If that's the case, then they are not really "believing" (trusting) in Jesus' death on the cross to be sufficient to save them. The Bible says that Jesus saves us "not on the basis of deeds which we have done in righteousness, but according to His mercy" (Titus 3:5). In addition to not trusting the Lord Jesus as their Savior, many people are like Satan in that they do not want God to rule over them. They want to control their own lives, so they do not trust Christ as their Lord. If that is true of you, "God is now declaring to men that all people everywhere should repent, because He has fixed a day in which He will judge the world in righteousness through a Man [Jesus Christ] whom He has appointed, having furnished proof to all men by raising Him from the dead" (Acts 17:30–31). Romans 10:9 tells us, "if you

confess with your mouth Jesus as Lord, and believe in your heart that God raised Him from the dead, you will be saved."

Assurance of Salvation

Many times when people are asked the question, "Do you know for sure that if you died you would go to heaven?" their answer is something like, "I'm not sure but I hope so." Because "knowing for sure" is such a critical issue, before you begin to answer the questions below, say a short prayer and ask God to show you the truth of His Word.

1. A person who is "saved" is going to heaven when he dies. What do you have to "do" to get "saved"?
   a. See John 3:16
   b. See Romans 10:13
   c. See John 1:12

2. Read the following verses and make a chart. On the left side, list what "saves" you and on the right side, list what will not "save" you:
   a. John 14:6
   b. Ephesians 2:8–9
   c. Acts 16:30–31
   d. Ephesians 2:4–5
   e. Colossians 1:13–14
   f. Galatians 1:3–4
   g. Titus 3:4–7

3. People think about their salvation in one of two ways: they must be good and do things to "earn" it, or Jesus did all the work necessary, and they must put their faith or "trust" in Him (alone) to be their Savior.

a. Nowhere does the Bible say that a person is saved by what he does or how good he is! On the contrary, the Bible says that the only acceptable sacrifice or punishment for sins is Jesus' sacrifice on the cross. Why, then, do so many people think they must believe in Jesus plus "earn" their way into heaven? Because it is logical from a human perspective. But God says, "For My thoughts are not your thoughts, nor are your ways My ways . . ." (Isa. 55:8). We're not holy, so we do not think as God thinks. Because He's holy, *all* sin must be punished. It is not enough for us to have done more good things than bad. All the bad had to be dealt with, and that's what Jesus declared when He said, "It is finished!"

b. Look up the following verses and write down what God wants you to know about assurance of your salvation.

1. Romans 3:28
2. Romans 8:1
3. Romans 10:11
4. John 5:24
5. John 6:47
6. 1 Corinthians 3:15
7. 2 Corinthians 1:9–10
8. 1 John 5:11–13
9. 1 Peter 1:3–5
10. Titus 1:2

4. There are basically three reasons why people don't have the assurance of their salvation:

a. They don't know what the Bible teaches, or they don't believe it.

b. They have never really put their trust in Jesus as their Lord and Savior. Jesus said, "But you do not believe because you are not of My sheep. My sheep hear My voice, and I know them, and they follow Me; and I give eternal life to them, and they will *never* perish; and no one will snatch them out of My hand" (John 10:26–28).

c. There is no evidence of salvation in their life such as a desire for God, a longing to please God, or obedience to Christ's commandments. "By this we know that we have come to know Him, if we keep His commandments" (1 John 2:3).

Salvation is a work of God, not a work of man. So if you are having doubts, ask God to grant you repentance from your sin and faith in His Son.

Notes

Chapter 3: What Do You Mean I Can Live without Him?

1. W. E. Vine, *Vine's Expository Dictionary of New Testament Words* (McLean: VA: Macdonald Publishing, nd.), 707.

Chapter 4: I'm Supposed to Respond *How?*

1. Special thanks to Lou Priolo for permission to adapt his material on manipulation for this chapter. To obtain Lou's CD, *How to Manage Manipulative People*, contact Pastoral Publications, P.O. Box 101, Wetumpka, AL, 36092. Tel. 866-437-0498.

Chapter 5: What Difference Does It Make *What* He Intended?

1. *Webster's Seventh New Collegiate Dictionary* (Springfield, MA: G. & C. Merriam, 1963), 406.

2. *New American Standard Exhaustive Concordance of the Bible,* (Nashville: Homan Bible Publishers, 1981), 7665.

3. Ibid., 3076.

4. For further information on church discipline, see Jay Adams's book, *The Handbook of Church Discipline* (Grand Rapids: Zondervan, 1986).

Chapter 6: Who Is the Fairest of Them All?

1. *Webster's Seventh New Collegiate Dictionary* (Springfield, MA: G. & C. Merriam, 1963), 981.

2. The following material about the daughters of Zion was adapted from material from Howard Dial of Berachah Bible Church in Fayette-ville, Georgia, with permission.

Chapter 7: Are You Sure PMS Is Real?

1. J. E. Daugherty, "Treatment Strategies for Premenstrual Syndrome," *American Family Physician* 58, no. 1 (July 1998): 183.

2. If you have any concerns about psychiatric drugs and whether you should take them or how to safely stop taking them, I recommend you read Dr. Joseph Glenmullen's book, *The Antidepressant Solution* (New York: Free Press, 2005).

Chapter 8: I Just Love Rules, Don't You?

1. Timothy George, *The New American Commentary, Galatians* (Nashville: Broadman and Holman, 1994), 96.

2. This material was adapted with permission from material by Howard Dial, pastor of Berachah Bible Church, Fayetteville, Georgia.

3. John MacArthur and Wayne Mack, *Introduction to Biblical Counseling* (Dallas: Word, 1994), 381–82.

4. The first four on this list were adapted from J. C. Ryles's book *Warnings to the Churches* (Edinburgh: Banner of Truth Trust, 1967), 62–66. This material was originally published in *Home Truths* and later in *Knots United* (first published in 1877).

Chapter 9: But What If I *Like* to Have My Ear Tickled?

1. Betty Friedan, *The Feminine Mystique* (New York: Dell, 1963), 79.

2. Ibid., 47.

3. Erik Erikson, *Identity: Youth and Crisis* (New York: W.W. Norton, 1968).

4. Friedan, *The Feminine Mystique*, 14.

5. Ibid., 77.

6. Justine Blau, *Betty Friedan, Feminist* (New York: Chelsea House, 1990), 47.

7. Friedan, *The Feminine Mystique*, 205.

8. Marilyn French, *The War against Women* (New York: Ballantine, 1992), 181.

9. Ibid., 55–56.

Chapter 10: You Want Me to Do What?

1. John Piper and Wayne Grudem, *Recovering Biblical Manhood and Womanhood* (Wheaton, IL: Crossway, 1991), 99, 102.

2. For more information on resources to protect a wife when her husband is sinning see Martha Peace, *The Excellent Wife* (Bemidji, MN: Focus, 1999), 155–73.

Chapter 11: Be Thankful? You Can't Be Serious!

1. This story was told with the permission of Lois Stride Green.

Appendix: Salvation Worksheets

1. These worksheets are reproduced with permission of Focus Publishing, Inc., Bemidji, MN, from the "Salvation Handbook," 2005.

Martha Peace was born, raised, and educated in and around the Atlanta area. She graduated with honors from both the Grady Memorial Hospital School of Nursing and Georgia State University. She has thirteen years' experience as a registered nurse, specializing in pediatric burns, intensive care, and coronary care.

She became a Christian in June of 1979. Two years later, Martha ended her nursing career and began focusing attention on her family and a ladies' Bible study class. For five years she taught verse-by-verse book studies. Then she received training and certification from the National Association of Nouthetic Counselors. NANC was founded by Jay E. Adams for the purpose of training and certifying men and women as biblical counselors. (For more information, visit www.nanc.org.)

Martha is a gifted teacher and exhorter. She worked for eight years as a biblical counselor at the Atlanta Biblical Counseling Center, where she counseled women. For the past several years, she has presented a workshop on various biblical counseling issues for women at NANC's annual conference. She also taught women's classes for six years at Carver Bible Institute and College, in Atlanta. Currently, Martha is a member of the adjunct faculty at The Master's College, in Valencia, California, teaching biblical counseling. She has authored four books: *The Excellent Wife, Becoming a Titus 2 Woman, Attitudes of a Transformed Heart*, and *Damsels in Distress*.

Martha is active with her family in Faith Bible Church in Peachtree City, Georgia, where she teaches a ladies' Sunday school class, sings in the choir, counsels women, and generally serves where needed. In addition, she conducts seminars for ladies' groups on topics such as "Raising Kids without Raising Cain," "The Excellent Wife," "Becoming a Titus 2 Woman,"

"Having a High View of God," and "Personal Purity." She speaks at a number of women's conferences each year both nationally and internationally.

Martha has been married to her high school sweetheart, Sanford Peace, for forty years. He is an air traffic controller with the FAA, but his real work is as an elder at Faith Bible Church. They have two married children and ten grandchildren.